Fresh Voices

COMPOSITION AT CAL POLY

2014–2015

Volume VIII

Edited by

Brenda M. Helmbrecht, Director of Writing

Assistant Editors:

Annie Garner • Jonathan Gotsick • Dawn Janke
Morgan Livingston • Chelsea Lynn • Rebekah Maples

HAYDEN
HM
McNEIL

Hayden-McNeil Sustainability

Hayden-McNeil's standard paper stock uses a minimum of 30% post-consumer waste. We offer higher % options by request, including a 100% recycled stock. Additionally, Hayden-McNeil Custom Digital provides authors with the opportunity to convert print products to a digital format. Hayden-McNeil is part of a larger sustainability initiative through Macmillan Higher Ed. Visit http://sustainability.macmillan.com to learn more.

Printed in the United States of America

10 9 8 7 6 5 4 3 2 1

ISBN 978-0-7380-6872-5

Hayden-McNeil Publishing
14903 Pilot Drive
Plymouth, MI 48170
www.hmpublishing.com

Helmbrecht 6872-5 F14

Contents

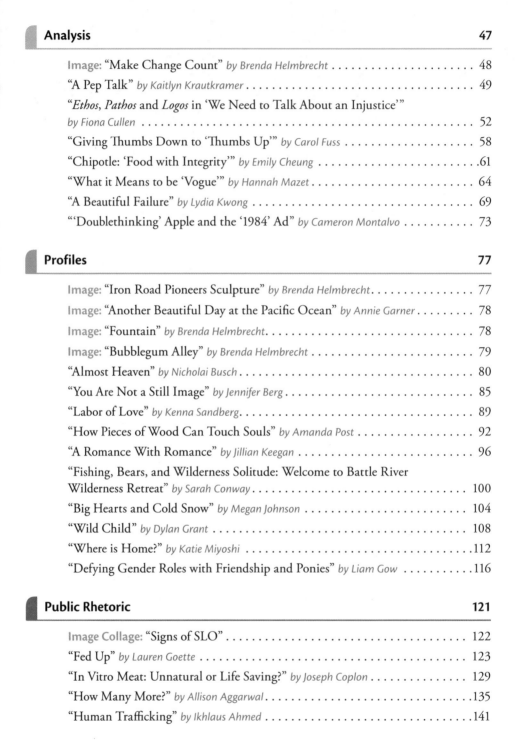

Appendices   175

Fresh Voices

Acknowledgements

The *Fresh Voices* editors would like to thank Dolores Lopez in the English Department for her help with essay submissions.

The editors would also like to thank the English Department and the College of Liberal Arts for supporting this project.

And, we also want to thank Cal Poly's English 133 and 134 students for submitting their work to this collection for the past seven years. Without your investment in your writing education, this collection would not be possible.

Front and Back Cover Images
"Spring at Laguna Lake" by Brenda Helmbrecht

Letter from the Director of Writing

Learn by Doing... and Learn by Writing...

Dear Student:

Welcome to *Fresh Voices*, a collection of writing that showcases the effort, commitment, and talent of last year's English 133 and 134 students.

The essays featured in the collection are typical of the intellectual engagement promoted in Cal Poly's first-year writing classes. We value the work of these writers for many reasons. The essays in this collection:

- take sophisticated approaches to the same assignments you are likely to meet in your composition courses.
- explore issues that matter most to students like you.
- use unique and interesting rhetorical strategies to engage their readers.
- have a distinct voice and style.

In short, these writers have something to say! Thus, we think they have something to teach you about writing at Cal Poly.

The selection committee did not select these essays because they earned "As" or because they are perfect (frankly, we don't know what grades these essays received and neither does your instructor). Moreover, our intention is not for you to imitate these essays in lieu of developing your own writing style and process. Instead, read the essays in this collection with an eye toward your own progress. Ask yourself, "What can these essays teach me about my own writing?" The essays in this collection will offer you new ways to approach your writing, perhaps in terms of how to craft an introduction, how to integrate quotations, or even how to develop and support your essay's thesis. Most importantly, these essays can help you bring greater complexity and depth to your writing—two traits that are highly valued in our composition courses.

> Ask yourself, "What can these essays teach me about my own writing?"

At the end of the collection, you will find important information about writing at Cal Poly. For instance, we have included information about campus resources that can provide additional support for your writing and research, including the University Writing and Rhetoric Center and Kennedy Library. I also encourage you to become familiar with the "Defining and Avoiding Plagiarism" section. And finally, at the end of the collection, you will find information for submitting your work to next year's *Fresh Voices*.

As the Director of Writing at Cal Poly, my job is to ensure that you receive progressive and innovative approaches to writing instruction. Indeed, one of Cal Poly's stated University Learning Objectives (ULO) is "effective communication," which means that you will be developing your writing skills throughout your Cal Poly career. You will soon find that writing at the college level requires you not only to demonstrate mastery of the skills you developed in high school, but also to develop new approaches to writing that you may not have tried before.

In my experience directing the writing program and teaching composition at Cal Poly, I have noted that students who stick with their "old" methods of writing—despite what they are learning in their college classes—tend to struggle the most in ENGL 133 and 134. For instance, you will be asked to write essays that move beyond the five-paragraph structure, or other formulaic approaches to writing, that you may have encountered in high school. You will be expected to select an organizational strategy that suits your topic, to use language and punctuation that most effectively conveys your meaning, to address your audience appropriately, and to select essay topics you care about.

Perhaps you have been waiting to exercise some creative control over your writing. If you commit to and reconnect with your writing, I predict that you will make incredible strides this year. **You will learn a lot by writing at Cal Poly!**

The selection committee and I welcome you to composition at Cal Poly!

> ## TIPS FOR SUCCESS
>
> - take advantage of the opportunity to revise.
>
> - spend time with your instructor's carefully considered feedback.
>
> - be prepared to receive assessments of your writing that are different in tone and purpose than the feedback you received in high school.
>
> - keep an open mind.
>
> - dismiss the notion that you write best under the pressure of time constraints.

Dr. Brenda M. Helmbrecht
Director of Writing

What to Expect in Your "Writing and Rhetoric" Course

TRANSITIONING FROM HIGH SCHOOL ENGLISH TO COLLEGE WRITING

You will likely see some overlap between the classes you took in high school and the composition classes you will take at Cal Poly. This is by design. English 133 and 134 are not intended to be complete departures from your high school courses. Rather, your college writing courses offer you an opportunity to build on the skills you have been developing for the past few years. You will be asked to complicate and challenge the ways you already think about writing.

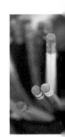

However, please know that even though you will find some overlap in terms of course content, your composition instructor's expectations will be different—perhaps higher. **In short, you will be held accountable for your rhetorical choices.** Your instructor will assume that when you write, you are making informed choices and s/he will determine and assess for the effectiveness of those choices. In effect, you won't just be regarded as a student. **You will be treated like a *writer*.**

In this new role, you will be expected to assume heightened responsibilities. In other words, you will need to attend class regularly, meet deadlines, and complete all of your coursework.

When in class, your instructor will assume that you will have something thoughtful and meaningful to contribute.

If you felt constricted in your high school English classes (sometimes timed-writing and high-stakes exams can dominate a course's focus), regard English 133 or 134 not as a class that you have to take, but as an opportunity to really improve your writing so you can successfully navigate the many writing projects you will encounter throughout your career at Cal Poly—including your senior project and the Graduation Writing Requirement (which is discussed in the "Appendices" section at the end of the collection).

COURSE CURRICULUM

While English 133/134 courses are shaped by the instructors' unique approaches to teaching writing, each section still tends to follow a parallel curriculum, thereby ensuring that each section meets the same learning objectives (which you can find in the appendices). While the papers you write in your course may not be exactly the same as the assignments described below, you will likely be writing papers that are comparable in purpose and approach to those presented in this collection.

Exploring Significant Moments

This essay is often written during the first week of the class, although some instructors require students to revisit and revise it again at the end of the quarter. In many of these essays, students reflect on their experiences as writers, drawing attention to the importance of developing a writing process, the challenges of writing, and the sense of accomplishment they experience after recognizing their development as writers. Other essays will explore a significant moment or experience in the writer's life that helped shape him/her.

Please note that these essays go beyond just telling a story: they each have a discernible focus and a purpose. Ultimately, these students are assessing their own abilities and experiences. On the one hand, you may find yourself nodding in agreement as you read these essays because you may have had similar experiences in your own life. On the other hand, you may be unable to directly relate to a particular writer's narrative—but, as a reader, your role is to *find* ways to connect with these writers' experiences. As you read, use these points of similarity and difference to help you consider your own experiences.

Profiling a Person, Place, Event, or Trend

In each of the profile essays included in this volume of *Fresh Voices*, students carved out distinctive approaches to the assignment—approaches that permitted them to explore exceptional elements found in cultures surrounding them. Topics for the profile sequence vary by instructor: some instructors select a theme, such as the environment or media; other instructors ask students to use this assignment to become better acquainted with an aspect of someone's life, a well-loved place, or even a social trend. For many instructors, conducting an effective interview—and learning how to accurately represent someone else's point of view—is an essential component of this essay.

You will find that this assignment challenges you to synthesize multiple texts and viewpoints: your analytic response to your interviewee's work, the interview itself, and, when appropriate, your own experiences and responses. If you choose to profile a place or a trend, you will also learn to incorporate field notes and other outside sources. In addition, you must account for and write to an audience that does not have knowledge of your essay's subject matter. In other words, you need to present your own "insider's perspective" about the profile subject. But remember: regardless of who or what you profile, this essay is created and shaped by you. In other words, your profile subject needs to speak *with* you as a writer, not *for* you.

Analysis

Learning how to analyze a text is one of the most important skills you will learn in English 133/134. Whether you are studying an advertisement or a speech, identifying the strategies an author/artist uses to persuade an audience helps you better understand how an argument is conveyed. In particular, your class will make a distinction between summary (what a text says) and analysis (how a text conveys its message). Breaking a text down to its individual parts helps you better understand how the text makes meaning for its readers.

While analytic papers can be composed individually, analysis is also part of every writing sequence in ENGL 133/134. For example, you may have to analyze your profile subject's work, environment, and thoughts. And, when writing your rhetoric paper (below), you will need to carefully analyze the evidence you use to support your claims.

Public Rhetoric and Argumentation

For this sequence, students choose a public issue and write a persuasive essay supporting their viewpoint on it. The persuasive essays in this collection cover a broad range of subjects. Yet you will see one common feature: the authors have a personal stake in their chosen topic.

In writing your own Public Rhetoric essay, you will learn that a well-written and fully supported argument requires you to conduct research both to support your own claims and to fairly depict opposing viewpoints. You will also learn to use the rhetorical appeals of *ethos*, *pathos*, and *logos* (defined on the following pages) to persuade and connect with your chosen audience. Regardless of the topic you choose, it's generally best to select a focus that matters to *you*, something you want to understand better and learn more about. Try not to approach your topic with a firmly held point-of-view; proving what you already *think* you know isn't the goal of this essay (indeed, it's important to understand the distinction between an opinion and an argument). Rather, as you conduct research and learn about your topic, your stance toward the topic may shift. Rhetorical inquiry and engagement requires this kind of flexibility.

Final Project

Each section of English 133/134 completes the course differently. Some classes conclude with presentations, others use portfolios, and some classes require unique projects like zines or a letter written to someone who can effect change in the world. Regardless of the kind of assignment you are given, it will require you to draw from everything you have been taught throughout the quarter. This assignment can be regarded as the capstone to the course in that it offers you an opportunity to demonstrate all that you have learned.

KEY COURSE CONCEPTS

Rhetoric

In its most basic terms, rhetoric generally refers to written, verbal, and visual persuasion. While you may have studied rhetoric in your high school English class, you will approach this concept through many different angles in your college writing classes.

According to Aristotle, rhetoric is the "ability to observe, in any given case, the available means of persuasion." In short, rhetoric refers to your ability to make effective choices when speaking and writing. Yet the word "observe" here is also key: it refers to your ability to look at how rhetoric is used *on* you, even when you are not consciously aware of it. With this definition in mind, you will study how rhetoricians—including you—persuade people to consider their point of view. Every time you sit down to write, you must account for the ways in which you want your audience to respond to your text. What means are available to you as you seek to persuade people to change their position on an issue? If you lose track of the rhetorical situation and forget to consider how to best communicate with and persuade your reader, your essay may not affect your readers the way you intend. In effect, every act of writing becomes an act of persuasion.

The Rhetorical Appeals

Throughout your ENGL 133/134 course, you will encounter three rhetorical concepts that may be new to you: *ethos, pathos,* and *logos.* We have borrowed these terms from Aristotle, who long ago argued that every writer who wants to communicate effectively with his or her audience must account for these appeals.

So when writing, make sure to account for the three rhetorical appeals:

Ethos: Credibility

When we use this term, we are simply talking about credibility. In other words, writers must develop a strong *ethos* for readers to regard the argument as credible. Audiences are most persuaded by writers who have the knowledge to write intelligently about a given subject, and audiences trust writers who present information accurately and fully. Conversely, they tend not to trust writers who leave out relevant information or who don't work with reliable sources. For instance, if a writer continually relies on web pages with no clear authors or publication dates (including Wikipedia), the argument may not be convincing. However, if a writer uses sources that have a track record of presenting information without a great deal of bias and that promote writers who conduct trustworthy research, the writer's *ethos* is increased and the audience is more likely to be persuaded.

Ethos can also be developed when writers simply share a relevant personal experience that gives them insider knowledge. So if you want to write an essay about water politics in California and your family owns a farm that struggles to obtain an adequate amount of water, it would make sense to share that information in your essay in order to build credibility as a writer. There are many ways to develop your *ethos*—some of them quite subtle. You will study these approaches in your course.

Pathos: Emotion

Readers are most invested in and persuaded by ideas to which they have a deep emotional connection. Even Aristotle, who believed rhetoric shouldn't rely on manipulating readers' emotions in order to persuade them, still conceded that a rhetorician will only be effective if s/he can garner some emotional response from the audience. Effective rhetorical moments, then, touch the reader on a deeper, emotional level. But the question is, *how* do you want your readers to feel? Moreover, how do you persuade a reader to feel as intensely about a subject as you do? In order to ensure that readers share your emotions when reading your work, you must first attempt to predict the elements that will encourage your readers to engage with your writing on an empathic or sympathetic level. When writing, you must account for the beliefs, values, and other personal attributes that may trigger an emotional response in your audience. Do you want your readers to feel anger? Frustration? Sadness? Joy? Do you want them to feel motivated to go out into the world and make changes? When deciding which words best convey your ideas, don't forget the emotional impact of language.

As a reader, you must also develop a critical awareness that enables you to determine if an argument overuses *pathos*. In other words, if an argument relies on your emotive response to persuade you and forgoes any other means of persuasion, you should be suspicious of it. The key here is balance. There is a fine line between persuasion and manipulation, but it's a distinction that every skilled rhetorician must make.

Logos: Reason

Though a piece of writing must make some use of *pathos*, emotions must still be balanced with logic. *Logos* refers to the entire structure of an argument. Does the argument overall make rational sense? Have you selected the kinds of sources that will encourage your reader to be persuaded by the logic of the argument? Perhaps you will want to look at scientific studies. Perhaps you can find some useful statistics to back up your ideas. But look for smaller ways to build a logical argument, too. For instance, using language like, "everyone knows…" automatically forces the reader to question your logic. After all, is there anything that "everyone knows"? Can you really account for everyone? As you conduct research and structure your essays, keep in mind that audiences like to see information presented rationally and logically.

Using the Three Appeals

You will learn that every effective paper has *ethos, pathos,* and *logos* coursing through it. However, some arguments—depending on their subject and purpose—may require that one appeal be stronger than the other two. For instance, if you are writing an argument about a highly technical subject, you may find yourself relying on *logos* more than *pathos.* Conversely, you can also find support for an argument that relies on all three appeals equally. For instance, you may find a statistic about Guiyu, China's electronic waste village. It's possible this one bit of evidence approaches the topic logically (*logos*), frustrates your reader (*pathos*), and, because the evidence is from a trustworthy, independent source, heightens your credibility (*ethos*).

©Hayden-McNeil, LLC

Aristotle defined rhetoric as the ability of "observing, in any given case, the available means of persuasion."

You will be able to use these appeals more effectively if you keep in mind the entire rhetorical situation, which can often be represented by **Aristotle's rhetorical triangle**:

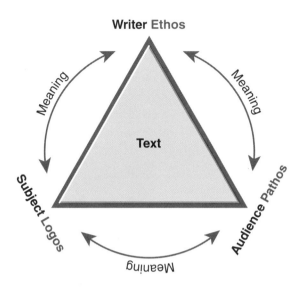

As you can see, the arrows here represent meaning. In other words, the rhetorical triangle tells us that a writer must account for the ways in which meaning moves back and forth between the three points—the writer, the subject, and the audience—simultaneously. Moreover, note that each arrow moves in two directions, indicating that meaning also moves in multiple directions (not just one direction). In other words, the audience you are writing for should influence how you present the subject, and both of those elements should influence your *ethos*. As you write, let these triadic relationships shape your text. After all, if you forget about your audience as you write and only focus on your subject and your *ethos*, your meaning will not be communicated in the way you intend.

Making Effective Rhetorical and Stylistic Choices

Too often, we think about writing only in terms of correctness. We become consumed with what's right and what's wrong and we forget that, as writers, we have control over our own writing choices. While there will certainly be an emphasis on grammar and mechanics in your composition course, you may be asked to think about these concepts through a stylistic lens.

"Style" can be regarded as a rhetorical concept that is less about error and more about the choices you make as a writer. In other words, you can make stylistic choices that break the rules. Yet, you must first understand the rules, and you need to account for how the choices you make affect the text and the reader (consult the rhetorical triangle above). For instance, we know that a fragment is not a complete sentence and that we generally need to write with complete sentences. But what if, for once, you don't want a complete sentence. Just a fragment. Is that okay?

What if you want a one-sentence paragraph?

Or what if you want to use "I"? Or you directly want to address the reader with "you"? Or what if you want to stop relying on commas and periods and instead want to try semicolons, colons, and dashes?

As you develop your writing style, work to make conscious, deliberate choices. Style is something writers work at; it's not innate. If a reader asks why you used a fragment, you need to be able to explain what effect you wanted that fragment to have. You will make good choices and some that are a little shaky—but that's okay. Style takes practice and, perhaps even more importantly, it requires you to take some risks with your writing. Sometimes the safest choice isn't the best one.

So turn off the grammar check and start making your own decisions!

Conducting an Interview

The key to conducting a good interview is to craft questions that enable you to capture your interviewee's candor and insights as fully as possible. As the interviewer, *you* are not the focus of the interview; rather, think of the interview in terms of collaboration and discussion. Try to meet with your subject in a setting that can reveal something about her profession, pastimes, or beliefs. You can set the tone for the interview by asking important questions when your subject is laughing, smiling genuinely, and just seems relaxed—moments when she is comfortable discussing tricky subjects. While uncompromising and unflinching questions can make for a dramatic essay, you still have a responsibility to approach your interviewee respectfully. Ideally, after the interview begins, get out of your subject's way and let her take hold of the interview by offering thoughtful responses to your carefully crafted questions.

While you can conduct an interview via phone or IM, it's best to be able to talk face-to-face. So if you are interviewing someone who is not in close proximity, try a video conferencing service, like "Skype," so you can track your interviewee's facial expressions and mannerisms.

How to Write Interview Questions

Writing questions for an interview can be tricky. Knowing which questions to ask and how to ask them makes all the difference. The following are five simple tips to help you write interview questions.

1. Avoid asking "double-barreled questions."

These questions actually hide multiple questions within them. For example the question, "Do you think he is telling the truth and that he deserves to be set free?" actually contains two questions. When asked double-barreled questions, the respondent will most likely just answer one of them and you may not get the information you seek. Thus, it's better to separate your questions.

2. Refrain from asking biased or leading questions.

Avoid asking questions that are slanted toward an opinion or viewpoint. A good interview question is neutral and allows the respondent to give his or her own take on an issue. Your question should not influence the respondent's opinion.

3. Avoid questions that assume a specific response.

Some questions have already assigned opinions to the interviewees. Note this question preceded by a statement: "A lot of people are angered by this crime. Are you one of them?" This question is structured in such a way that an issue is painted as a crime when it probably still needs to be proven. You can secure this same information by simply asking, "Do you believe a crime took place?"

4. Keep your questions short and clear.

Sometimes brevity is key. Long, detailed questions may confuse your subject and you may not get a detailed response in return. Write questions that are short and concise. The stylistic choices you make are essential too; the slightest grammatical or punctuation mistake can change a question's meaning.

5. Ask questions beginning with WHY, HOW, WHAT, and WHEN.

Your interview won't actually reveal much information if you rely on questions that elicit "yes" or "no" as a response. Devise open-ended questions to which you don't know the answer. Give your subject space to think carefully and thoughtfully about a question. And be prepared to go off script and ask follow-up questions if you want to know more about your subject's responses.

Learning to ask carefully crafted, thoughtful questions is a life skill that will benefit you in your classes, in job interviews, and in conversations with interesting people. As you develop interview questions for any research project, keep in mind your own credibility (*ethos*) as an interviewer. What steps do you need to take to:

- Present yourself professionally?
- Appear confident and relaxed?
- Establish trust with your subject?

LOOK HERE

Some advice from a pro...

In his recently published *New Yorker* article, John McPhee discusses his experiences interviewing people during a fifty-year career as a journalist. He advises:

> If I am in someone's presence and attempting to conduct an interview, I am wishing I were with Kafka on the ceiling. I'd much rather watch people do what they do than talk to them across a desk. I've spent hundreds of hours in the passenger seats of their pickups, often far from pavement, bouncing from scribble to scribble. Under a backpack, and hiking behind environmentalist David Brower, I walked across the North Cascades, up and down the switchbacks, writing in a notebook...

> Whatever you do, don't rely on memory. Don't even imagine that you will be able to remember everything verbatim in the evening what people said during the day.... From the start, make clear what you are doing and who will publish what you write. Display your notebook as if it were a fishing license. While the interview continues, the notebook may serve other purposes, surpassing the talents of a tape recorder. As you scribble away, the interviewee is, of course, watching you. Now, unaccountably, you slow down, and even stop writing, while the interviewee goes on talking. The interviewee becomes nervous, tries harder, spills out the secrets of a secret life, or maybe just a clearer and more quotable version of what was said before. (50)

Work Cited

McPhee, John. "Elicitation." *The New Yorker*. April 7, 2014. (50–57). Print.

You can find McPhee's entire article here:

> http://www.newyorker.com/reporting/2014/04/07/140407fa_fact_mcphee

Writing with Images

"Pictures are supposed to be worth a thousand words.
But a picture unaccompanied by words may not mean anything at all.
Do pictures provide evidence? And if so, evidence of what?
And, of course, the underlying question: do they tell the truth? [...]
A captionless photograph, stripped of all context, is virtually meaningless.
I need to know more."

Errol Morris, Documentary Filmmaker
"Liar, Liar, Pants on Fire," The New York Times.

We are bombarded by images every day. We laugh at memes on our Facebook pages and Twitter feeds, and traverse fantasy worlds in our video games. In fact, we encounter image-based modes of communication on television, online news and gossip sites, and

> ### LOOK HERE
>
> To read Errol Morris's essay on the relationship between captions and images, check out his "Opinionator Blog" at the *New York Times*:
>
> **http://opinionator.blogs.nytimes.com/category/errol-morris/**

films *so often* that we may not even pause to ask critical questions: Who created these images? Whose agenda do these images serve? How I should I respond?

Analyzing visual rhetoric allows us to understand both the explicit and implicit arguments that images make about culture and society. Many people wrongly regard the act of examining an image as an effortless process, assuming that only a casual, quick glance is required. The sheer pervasiveness of images seems to place them outside the reach of critical reflection and analysis. Writing, on the other hand, is often seen as requiring careful planning and decision making to become effective. However, visuals and writing have much in common: they are intricately bound as they seek to entertain, to educate, and to persuade. Additionally, readers may not be persuaded by written arguments alone; thus, when an image is effectively paired with text, the reader may get a fuller understanding of an issue. Understanding how images persuade will enable you to approach the images you encounter with a greater critical eye.

Writing with Images

As members of a visual culture, we must learn how to navigate, interpret, and analyze the messages conveyed to us via imagery. Many English 133/134 instructors ask students to study images through a rhetorical lens, which means that students explore how images make rational arguments (*logos*), how they evoke an emotional response from a viewer (*pathos*), and how (when used effectively) images can enhance a writer's or speaker's credibility (*ethos*).

As you read *Fresh Voices*, focus on the relationship between the images and the writing. How do the images you see enhance the written arguments? How do the visuals heighten appeals to *ethos*, *logos*, and *pathos*? What meaning can you glean from the images presented in this collection?

NOTE

The following two art projects were originally featured in Cal Poly's "University Art Gallery." This year *Fresh Voices* partnered with the art gallery with the intention of highlighting visual art created by Cal Poly students.

The Art Gallery is located in Dexter (Building 34), next to the library. It's open Tuesday–Saturday, 11–4. For further information, contact Jeffrey Van Kleek, the Gallery Coordinator. You can find the Gallery's website here:

http://www.artgallery.calpoly.edu/index.php

The College Appetite Dilemma
Artwork by Jessica Ferguson

Jessica is an Art and Design major.

Artist's Note: Life is a rollercoaster ride that is full of constant decision-making. One of the choices you have to make each day is what type of food you are going to put into your body. Now I don't know about you, but I absolutely love delicious food. I don't see myself as one who strictly eats healthy or not healthy; rather, I am an individual who tries to balance the two. Although, living on a college campus as a freshman has definitely thrown off my balance. Junk food and unhealthy snacks tend to be more practical and readily available throughout my busy schedule. So I lean towards junk food.

While those bright red licorice pieces might look irresistible and mouth watering, is eating them really worth it in the long run? Most of the time I eat junk food when I am tired

(continued)

and stressed. Ironically, processed food only increases my sense of depression and stress. Junk food has a short-term effect when more natural foods fuel my brain and give me more energy.

Food photography has always been an interest to me. Food has so many wonderful textures and variations that create really unique images. Since this is a black and white photography project, I focused on the different contrasts and textures in a range of food products. My photographs are a physical reminder that for every unhealthy food there is something out there that tastes just as good, and is much better for your body and health overall. I will leave you with this thought: you are what you eat, so choose wisely.

CONSIDER THIS

- In this original art piece, Ferguson asks viewers to reflect on their dietary choices by pairing junk food with fruits and vegetables. Is her approach persuasive? Is she making a logically sound argument (*logos*)? Do you think the image's claim is clear? In other words, what argument does this image make?

- In her artist's note, Ferguson addresses her work's aesthetics, noting that she used black and white photography to "[focus] on the different contrasts and textures in a range of food." How would you describe the texture of these objects? Do the shades of black, white, and grey change how you normally respond to this food, which would normally appear in a broad array of vibrant colors?

LOOK HERE

Staying fit requires a healthy diet, and the many local farmers' markets help make that possible. You can find a schedule here: **http://www.slocountyfarmers.org/**

However, physical activity is also key. While the Cal Poly Recreation Center provides students with an excellent space for physical fitness, the San Luis Obispo community offers many prospects for students who prefer to exercise outdoors. For more information on hiking, biking, and kayaking, look here:

https://www.centralcoastoutdoors.com/index.asp

Not Alone
Artwork by Morgan Momsen

Morgan is an Art and Design major.

Artist's Note: This series was part of a final assignment for my black and white photography class. For each photograph, I asked the person, "What is the meanest thing someone has said to you?" They wrote their answers on transparencies and I printed their words on top of their portraits. I titled this piece "Not Alone" because I wanted people to know that even though you might feel isolated when bullied, others have been in your position, and you are truly not alone. At first it was challenging to get people to share, but as I moved forward with the project, more and more people were willing to contribute because they knew they were not alone.

CONSIDER THIS

- Momsen's piece asks her audience not only to reflect on the damaging comments they have heard from people, but also to reflect on how *they* have treated the people in their lives. Careless, offhand comments—as well as targeted insults—can have long-lasting effects on people's lives. As you study these photographs, what moments in your life come to mind? Can these images change how you interact with both strangers and close acquaintances in your own life?

- What argument is Momsen making with the art piece? How does she use *ethos*, *pathos*, and *logos*?

- How does the text affect how you respond to the images? In other words, how might you respond to the text without the images, and how might you respond to the images without the sentiments written across them?

LOOK HERE

There are many national organizations committed to ending bullying. For instance, stopbullying.gov provides a "Lifeline" for victims of bullying (1-800-273-TALK). If someone in your life is the victim of bullying, seek out resources to help them find the support they may need.

A project similar to Momsen's was started on tumblr by a group of Harvard students who wanted to "[highlight] the faces and voices of black students at Harvard College." You can find the project, titled, "I, too, am Harvard," here:

http://itooamharvard.tumblr.com/

Which moments have shaped you as a writer? As a student? As a person?

Being open to new experiences, beliefs, cultures, and new ways of thinking is an essential component of college life. Your shifting perspectives may also require you to think about language in new ways. As you prepare for this sequence, which relies on narration and description, consider the narratives in your life that helped shape you. The following essays and images present important moments—both grand and small in scale—in the writers' lives.

SLO Flow in Orange

I was walking home from campus with music streaming through my headphones on a sunny spring day. It was one of those days when I felt immense gratitude for all aspects of my life: personal, family, work. I call those moments "SLO Flow" moments; you know, everything is just moving along smoothly. As I crossed the street and turned the corner, I was greeted with blooming flowers and fresh oranges at the bottom of a neighbor's driveway. The colors popped and the message of "help yourself" spoke to me on a couple of levels: first, the literal

Photo and narration by Dawn Janke

neighborly giving was touching and added to the SLO Flow; and second, the notion of helping yourself confirmed what for me has been clear lately, that we are all responsible for our own bright spots in life, especially when we're open to seeing the bright side.

Study the image. What kind of narratives can you draw out of it? What questions does this image raise for you? Can you use this simple image of a box of free oranges to tell a story? Can you locate a similar story in your own life?

Photos and narration by Jeff Van Kleek

Our "Little Free Library"

I built my "Little Free Library" after reading about it in *On Wisconsin*, the University of Wisconsin, Madison alumni magazine. My neighborhood [in SLO] was slowly turning from college students to families with small children. Once the library was up, my kids painted it, each having a side to make their masterpiece. We filled it with books and waited.

Slowly and organically the library became a regular stop for people around the block. Families stop with small ones in wagons or training wheels. Older kids stop by on skateboards and bikes. The retirement homes near me produce a steady influx of older readers and their books. It has become a focal point for our neighborhood and conversation starter for people meeting new people. I have talked about it with people from Maine to North Carolina to just down the road.

Our library is no longer my own. We are only curators. We look to make sure the books' spines are faced out for easy identification. We make sure there are enough children's books. And we read books left by visitors.

LOOK HERE

Read the *On Wisconsin* Van Kleek refers to:

http://onwisconsin.uwalumni.com/features/
its-a-mailbox-its-a-bird-house-no-wait-its-a-library/

CONSIDER THIS

- What do the images of the library and the oranges have in common? Can you find any visual or narrative themes? In other words, do they tell similar stories?

The Color of Empathy

Christian Ulrichsen

Reflective Memo: *This was the first essay I had written in a long time, as I took a couple years off after high school. But I found that, as I started to write, it came to me a lot more easily than it had when I was in high school. Now I really enjoy creative writing, something I didn't know until I took English 134.*

A low rumbling filled my head as I opened my eyes and rubbed the sleep out of them. "Barbara Ann" by The Beach Boys spilled softly out of the stereo. I peeled the seatbelt off of my face and looked over to one of my sisters, who promptly removed the lollipop from her mouth and blurted out, "Are we there yet?"

"We're officially in Half Moon Bay," replied my dad softly, so as not to wake my mom in the passenger seat, "It shouldn't be more that 15 minutes now."

I turned my head to the window and gazed outside. As my focus drifted beyond the huge farms that rushed past us and the hills that lay behind them, the vivid colors of the landscape swirled together and became smeared paint on an endless canvas. Blue, green, yellow, and red flowed past one another before my eyes. Suddenly, something drew my focus away from things that were beyond my vision and I took a closer look at the fields that lay before me. Littered amongst the acres of green were countless colorless forms moving slowly about. I strained my eyes and pressed my face up against the glass, but I could not see what these things were until we drove close enough to one that I was able to make out some level of detail. It was a person: a man, on his hands and knees, pulling crops out of the earth. He looked so tired, his hands covered in dirt and his face beaten by the wind and the sun. I turned away from the window and stared at the floor for the rest of the trip. Finally, we reached our destination, a large red and white house that towered over the surrounding homes. My dad took the key out of the ignition and turned around to face my sisters and me. "Welcome to your new home, kids," he said, "Be sure to take off your shoes before you go inside."

Living in a new town was not easy. Not only did I have to start a new life, but I had to adjust to all the changes that middle school brought as well. I had a lot of difficulty making new friends and had to change schools a few times because I was failing most of my classes. I simply could not accept this place as my home. To me, Half Moon Bay had stolen me away from everything I knew. It seemed as if the whole town was perpetually gray, as though the thick fog that frequently crawled in from the ocean stained all it touched with its dull, lifeless color. Whenever we passed the fields as we drove in and out of town, I would look out the window at the people hunched over the crops and see that they, too, had been stained gray by the heavy fog.

In seventh grade, I ended up attending a private school named Seacrest where the classes were small and I could receive extra support and attention from my teachers. One day, the lesson in our English class was about empathy. My teacher described empathy as "the ability to put yourself in someone else's shoes."

"There is an essay due Friday," she said, and a collective moan rose from the classroom, "I want you to write about someone else's life, as though you were that person."

The computer screen stared blankly at me as I struggled to think of who I could possibly base my essay on. I did not yet have any friends in my class, so I certainly could not write about one of them. Members of my family were out of the question as well, obviously, since they were all totally lame. My mind wandered to the many people I so often saw toiling in the fields nearby and it struck me: I could write my paper about one of them!

After "inventing" a character for my story, I closed my eyes and tried to imagine myself as this person I had created in my mind. Sharp images rushed into my head and I was transported out of my house. I was Carlos, an illegal immigrant and father of four, two of which were born on American soil. *Two years ago, I spent every penny I had and risked my own life as well as those of my children and*

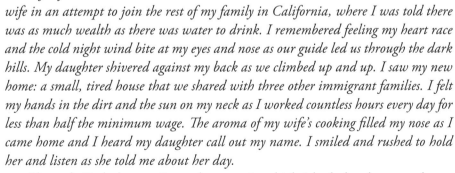

LOOK HERE

To learn more about immigrant farm workers, check out the "Immigrant Farm Workers Congressional Hearing" where Stephen Colbert recounts his experiences working just one day in the fields:

https://www.youtube.com/watch?v=ewPburLEZyY

wife in an attempt to join the rest of my family in California, where I was told there was as much wealth as there was water to drink. I remembered feeling my heart race and the cold night wind bite at my eyes and nose as our guide led us through the dark hills. My daughter shivered against my back as we climbed up and up. I saw my new home: a small, tired house that we shared with three other immigrant families. I felt my hands in the dirt and the sun on my neck as I worked countless hours every day for less than half the minimum wage. The aroma of my wife's cooking filled my nose as I came home and I heard my daughter call out my name. I smiled and rushed to hold her and listen as she told me about her day.

Through Carlos's eyes, I saw the town in which I had already spent almost two years of my life. For Carlos, everything in Half Moon Bay was beautiful. The town was not a miserable shade of gray. Instead, every color was vivid and alive, every day spent in this place was a gift. Words and emotions flowed out of me onto the screen and before I knew it I was finished. I read what I had just written and realized that I was looking at my situation all wrong. Something about the way I thought needed to change.

It was the first paper I ever received praise for in my life. My teacher read it out loud in front of the entire class and my peers came up to tell me how interesting my essay was, how they had never thought of it that way before. As I looked about I saw that the colors around me now were just as brilliant as they were when I saw them through Carlos's eyes. The sky was as blue as it had ever been, the grass greener than I even remembered. I saw that the fog that coated the town on occasion had never actually soaked into my surroundings, that the only things stained by the fog were my own eyes.

Christian Ulrichsen is a Biochemistry major.

CONSIDER THIS

- Analyze the essay's title. How does it contribute to the meaning of the essay as a whole?

- Empathy can be a powerful rhetorical tool. How can you use empathy in both your persuasive writing and in your daily interactions?

The Great Escape

Isamar Hernandez

Reflective Memo: *This essay is a reflection of why I love to write. When I was writing this essay, I thought about how my love for writing only increased after the event depicted. It was a bit hard to write this essay. I kept thinking back to what I went through and there were times when I reconsidered the topic. Ultimately, however, I decided to write about how writing saved my life because I felt that it explains my passion and who I have become. My goal is to have this essay published because I feel like others should be able to read this and know that if ever the need arises, reading and writing can become an escape from reality.*

I have always been a writer. From kindergarten, to present day, I have loved to write. There was a time, however, when writing became more of a lifeline than a pastime. Writing became my anchor to sanity, and I held on with everything I had. Had it not been for the journal I kept and the stories and poetry I wrote, I might not be sitting here, writing this essay.

The beginning of high school was marked by a scary transition. That summer, I had become involved in my first romantic relationship. My father, who had been the breadwinner of the family, suddenly saw himself without a job. My mother, who had often been home, had to take extra hours at work to keep up with expenses. There were so many changes to my life that year, and this was just the beginning. My father's lack of work drove him to a dark depressive state that would affect my family for several months. He was on edge all the time and his temper was short and fiery. My mom was never home to see this side of him. I became the target of this temper, and my life became a living hell. The abuse I dealt with was unbearable. I could not fathom the idea of a father that could be so cruel.

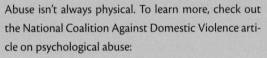

LOOK HERE

Abuse isn't always physical. To learn more, check out the National Coalition Against Domestic Violence article on psychological abuse:

http://www.ncadv.org/files/PsychologicalAbuse.pdf

I became immersed in literature. I learned to block the world and my problems via reading. I lost my friends because of the shame I dealt with, so books became my only friends. It was a total cliché. I began to write like I had never before. I kept various journals, each with their own story. One journal was about daily life. Another was all for poetry. My favorite journal, however, was the one where my dreams and fantasies took life. I wrote about the love I wanted to find, about the parents I wanted to have, about the life I so desperately wanted to escape. In my writing, I could be the person I wanted to be, live the life I wanted to live, and dream as much as I wanted to. Life had become hard, but life had also made me a dreamer. I dared to dream in the pages of my journal and suddenly, I had hope. I could express my discontent with my parents at my will's desire. I could be a heroine, or a damsel in distress. I could love or fight. Above all, I could talk about the situation at home and not be afraid of retaliation. I could confide in my journals my worries, my fears, my hatred, and my solitude.

I held onto my journals as I had never held on to anything before. I was in a deep depression myself when I was presented with the opportunity to submit a short story for a contest that the library was hosting. The topic was about obstacles that we were going through or had overcome. The prize was a free membership to the book club and the story posted in the library. I did not have to think very much to know that this was my opportunity to have my voice

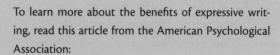

LOOK HERE

To learn more about the benefits of expressive writing, read this article from the American Psychological Association:

http://www.apa.org/monitor/jun02/writing.aspx

heard and my story told. I decided that I would submit a piece I had already written about what I was going through. It was written as a fairytale with no happy ending. Instead of living happily ever after, the main character took her own life because she could no longer face her fears. The title was that of this essay, "The Great Escape."

A few days after I submitted the piece I was called into the principal's office. Upon entering his office, I saw that there were several people in the room. My teachers, the librarian, counselors, my parents, all sat teary eyed, their heads hung. They wanted to talk to me about my piece. Although it had won, they were concerned about its content. My mother could not believe that this had been going on, or that I felt the way I did. I was put under a close watch by the administration and my father was reprimanded for his actions, for while it had not been physical abuse, his words were what tore my soul apart.

In a sense I felt that writing had saved my life. Had it not been for the submission of that piece, I might have ended up like the girl in my story. Had I not written, no one would have known of my troubles and my life's struggles. Since then, I have kept writing, but now with the purpose of entertainment. I love to write stories that I, as a reader, would enjoy. I hope to keep writing throughout my life so that maybe one day my writing can serve as an escape for someone who like me, struggled to keep hope alive.

Isamar Hernandez is an Agricultural Communications major.

Consider This

- Think about your own life experiences: have you ever used writing as a kind of therapy? If not, how could writing be a helpful form of expression?

- At one point, the writer mentions her immersion in literature/writing "was totally cliché." There might be moments when clichés can move an essay forward; yet, clichés also can get in the way of meaning. Can you find an example of a cliché in this essay? How does this cliché function?

To The Deep End

Jacob Hinshaw

Writing is, in some ways, a paradox. Professionals and statisticians claim that an overwhelming percentage of communication has absolutely nothing to do with the words we choose to use—essentially, we communicate without the necessity of a precise vocabulary. And yet, from the moment we can grip a crayon to the day we finished formalized schooling, we are bombarded with the notion that we must express ourselves on a page to be successful (even when, in a classroom these attempts are regularly feeble, rushed, and half-hearted.) Writer's voice or no, it feels a tad bit confusing.

Naturally, an opposing side exists; others argue that writing is immensely therapeutic. To a degree, I understand this, and do not intend to dispel such concepts. I instead choose to find my therapy through friendships. As has been made apparent to me over a lifetime of searching for intimacy with others, developing relationships is not an immediate process. So, while I generally attempt a sincere and kind attitude, my three closest friends are those I've known the longest: James, Jack, and Anthony. Though on paper they are just names, to me they are truer and dearer than the paltriness of words can convey. I have come to appreciate the closeness found only in true intimacy between friends through a lifetime of struggles, successes and failures with them at my side.

As a brief aside, I would like to acknowledge that I try to avoid cynicism. I do not endure the struggles of starvation, perpetual disease, poverty, nor any other life-threatening standard of living. I have been afforded innumerable luxuries since the day I was born and I take time to appreciate them as often as I can. As for my difficulties…let it suffice to say that they are few and far between. My most troublesome trouble is not even entirely my own. It belongs to parents, friends, and entire family, and most of all, to my best friend. Who wants to kill himself.

> **LOOK HERE**
>
> If you, or someone you know, is struggling with depression or suicidal thoughts, consider contacting Cal Poly's Health and Counseling Services. They can provide you with the resources you need.
>
> **http://www.hcs.calpoly.edu**

He's nineteen years old, the same age as me. Compared to our grandparents, such an age is almost laughable. To adults, he has his whole life ahead of him, just a boy, worlds of experience waiting for him, people to see, places to be, love, life, learning. Except he doesn't want to love, live, or learn. He doesn't want any of it.

Personally, I hope to be married some day (I've got three takers as to date), and I sincerely hope (God-willing) I'll raise a family; every Christmas I'll drive home to my mother and father from that new life I've made for myself, simply giddy with all the experience I've gained by making my way in this world, positively teeming with fanciful anecdotes about Bill from the office and those rambunctious next-door neighbors. Granted, that's not the path everyone envisions for themselves—and, might I add, my cliché ideal is far from set in stone—but for the most part, a majority of the populous that is my age group anticipates some brightness for their future.

And that is precisely why clinical depression happens to be such an astronomical bitch. When you're depressed, you don't get to think about tomorrow as a good things, even though it's going to be your eighteenth birthday and your friends have thoughtfully bought you presents (those heavy with shared memories in which you laughed till you cried). While everyone stands around you laughing at a slightly distasteful but undeniably witty joke, you have to feign interest and conjure up a faux smile, plastered on your face so no one around you knows what you force yourself to hold back. You'll keep it all inside, because no one needs to bear the burden of knowing that every day, you simply don't want to exist anymore.

You want to die.

Now, of course, the severity of my word choice, and the above specifics I provide, might (conceivably) suggest that I hold knowledge on depression—the kind powerful enough to drive a person to kill himself—knowledge granted only by personally living within its chokehold. Let me point out, as a simple matter of clarification, that I do not now, nor have I ever, wanted to take my own life. It is instead in the eyes of my friend that I have seen and lived these horrors. Whether it was across a computer screen, a cell phone, or listening face to face, I suffered with him as he fought through his mood swings—ranging from rampant self-hatred to complete indifference—my entire senior year, alongside other close friends. As I listened to the intricacies of a pain-twisted mind, it slowly became clear that it was a mind I did not know.

We met outside of school, texted late into the night, used Internet chat until four o'clock in the morning, every moment of conversation slowly crystallizing in my mind that he had given up. His hopelessness was infectious and seemingly incurable, and for a long time, "getting better" felt impossible, like fighting against a relentless current. It was exhausting. *Exhausting.* More than that, I began to question our friendship. Did the childhood friend I'd known and loved remain, or had this disease, this plague, already taken him while he was still here?

Doctors and therapists explained the disconnect in the chemical pathways of his mind, but it was always just words. A rehearsed set of clever syntax, prepared and delivered for the hundredth time. These idiots talked about him as if he were some machine. They made him out to be a robot with circuitry to be examined, diagnosed, and treated in a mechanical fashion, not a human being who lives in constant emotional agony. Their false empathy was sickening. Eventually, he was checked into a psych ward because he was a *danger to himself.* So when these people would talk at me—"sympathetically" explaining what was happening in his mind and how treatable everything was—I'd cross my arms, lean back, smile politely, and patiently wait for them to shut up.

I've lost people before: grandparents, friends of family, acquaintances. I've been to school seminars about suicide awareness. I fully recognize death as a part of life; it's unavoidable and it comes in many forms. But now, when it's someone my age and it's a disease that's been cured before, I can't get my head around it. It's so foreign—so impossible. When you're nineteen, it can't be, literally *cannot* be "your time to go," because your time has barely even started. What does that even mean? "It's just their time" feels like some copout bullshit excuse when no one has an explanation for why someone's dying. And even though he's still here, it's like someone grabbed his egg timer when it was still on 56 seconds and is trying to wrench it down to zero. And it's *him.* He's the one doing it. Now, friends and family all hold our breath until it goes off, but we're blindfolded and so we just have to wait until the bell rings.

And that's just it, really. I'm waiting. For a phone call. I'm waiting for a phone call that I can't prepare myself for. When I answer, I won't be ready, and after I hang up…

I won't recover.

Regardless of the dozens of medications he downs or the hours of therapy he endures, it's a reality that I've been preparing for. Outside of my denial, I know he's not getting any better.

And so that's it. I've moved through some arbitrary ordering or words and phrases that academia hopefully wouldn't frown upon.

So where's my resolution?

Jacob Hinshaw is an Architectural Engineering major.

CONSIDER THIS

- Hinshaw works with some very difficult subject matter in this essay. If you choose to work with personal subjects in your own work, it's important to keep in mind your audience. In other words, you will receive feedback on all of your writing in ENGL 133/134, so attempt to select subject matter that you feel comfortable sharing, as Hinshaw has.

- How would you describe Hinshaw's conclusion? Does he wrap everything up neatly? Or does his conclusion feel a little more open-ended? Is his approach satisfying to you as a reader?

A Gift From Beyond

Rachel Smith

My grandfather and I had a running joke for a few years from when we were on vacation until he died. On one foggy August morning off the coast of Northern California in a tiny town named Mendocino, an elderly man with a long white beard and an even longer ponytail in the back (he resembled a hippie Santa Claus) and his wife were walking the bluffs and saw a tattered piece of blue cloth, only partially visible through the dirt. As he bent down to get a better look, he heard the crack of 70-year old knees, and when he came back up he was holding a finger puppet dressed in a blue robe with crown on its head—a king! He returned from his walk and entered the house, proclaiming he'd found a king. The rest of us were as groggy as the weather, and just stared at him, confused. Still puzzled about what he was doing, we watched as my grandmother brought him a white lace doily, which he draped over an old rusty candleholder. He then placed the dirty finger puppet on top of the "throne" he had fashioned. For the rest of our vacation, he would make references or jokes about "The King," jokes that continued well after the vacation since he brought "The King" home with him.

Thinking myself quite clever, I scoured over children's toy stores until I found the perfect Christmas gift for my grandfather—a queen for his king. She wore a bright pink dress which flowed like water down one of those fake hotel waterfalls, and had a light brown wooden head, sanded so round it was as smooth as plastic, with a golden tiara on top. Finally, it was Christmas, and I was dancing with anticipation for him to open my gift. As he tore the red and green striped wrapping paper off my present, a huge smile cracked on his face, and his laugh jingled through the living room, instantly drawing all eyes on him. While everyone else found it funny, and groaned about not encouraging him, I knew he loved it, and that it meant a lot to him.

At one point I stole the king and queen, mailing my grandfather a picture of the two royals bound together by a shoelace, with the cold steel of a knife at their throats. On a trip to visit my grandfather, he surreptitiously rescued the king and queen from captivity; this started a war of hide-and-seek between the two of us, and the two royal puppets. However, on one trip to my grandparents' house, my patience had run out, and I gave up searching for the "king" and "queen." I later learned that not only had my search come up empty handed, but my grandfather had forgotten where he had hidden them. Even with my grandmother's help it seems they were lost. After a while, I had all but forgotten about the puppets, and when I did think about them they didn't seem important anymore—after all, I was growing up and definitely no longer a child.

When I eventually realized how old my grandfather actually was, he got very sick. We found out he had pancreatic cancer, but at the time I didn't think it was a big deal because I knew there was chemo, and besides, my uncle once had cancer but got better, so why wouldn't grandpa? My grandmother was older and had more health problems than grandpa, so I knew he would be okay. I was wrong, though, and as the disease ravaged his body he became so gaunt that he looked like he was made out of wax. It took less than a month from his diagnosis to his death.

Only two weeks later, we had to have our first Christmas without him. We continued the day as we normally would, but the whole thing had a morbid undertone. The family was all upset, but of course my grandmother was particularly devastated which made each of us feel worse. During present opening everyone realized that we each had a rectangular gift with the tags written in my grandfather's handwriting; with some curiosity mixed with caution we all opened our gifts. With hesitation, I slowly unwrapped the present, feeling my stomach shrinking with nervous anticipation. Inside was a clear, plastic box with an "I love you" sticker on the front, and the king and queen inside. I immediately felt my face growing hot, and tears streaming down my face. My thoughts ranged from *I can't believe he found them* to *I can't believe he's not here to laugh and share this with me*; it was a heart-wrenching moment—I was wallowing in despair over his death and at the same time I realized right then how fast things can change in life and that I needed to cherish what's important because you just never know when they'll be gone forever.

> **LOOK HERE**
>
> Otherwise ordinary objects can often mean the most to us, an idea explored in this documentary about families of 9/11 victims:
>
> **http://video.pbs.org/program/objects-and-memory/**

This tragedy pulled my family closer together, and pulled my grandmother into the center. Throughout my childhood she had always been in the background while my grandfather was the center. While the "King and Queen" had been reconnected with the outside world, my grandmother would not be reconnected until the afterlife. My grandfather's passing made me realize I had never really been that close with my grandmother, and that I wanted to be before she was gone, too. For the past few years I would drive down to my grandmother's house and drive her places and do chores for her, and just keep her company. In this time we have grown close, and we talk every Sunday now that I am away at college. I see now that while the "King" was the main figurehead, the "Queen" still mattered and played an important role in the joke; my grandmother still mattered. Becoming close with my grandmother was the silver lining in the deep grief of losing my grandfather.

Rachel Smith is a History major.

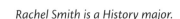

CONSIDER THIS

- Which rhetorical appeals (*ethos*, *pathos*, and/or *logos*) does the writer use to connect with her audience?

- If you were to write a piece about an object that holds particular importance to you, what would it be? Why? How would you describe it and narrate its significance?

Exploring Significant Moments

Have You Ever Heard of a Louisiana Tree Dog?

Alexa Batta

In the summer of 2010, my naïve 16-year-old self made a fateful trip to Louisiana. A trip made memorable, not by the miles traveled, the crazy people encountered, or the unusually painful Cajun food ingested, but by the purchase of a scraggly little puppy named Kevin Kerby Houghs. I didn't know it then, but that $27.00 puppy would become the best dog I ever had.

not strong

It all started at a truck stop in Bayou Cane, Louisiana. I had driven all the way from Arizona by myself to deliver a buffalo to a man with a questionable amount of intelligence, but that's another story. After completing "Operation Buffalo Drop," I was refueling my truck, about to make the long journey home, when I met a man like no one I had ever seen before. He was one of the several gas station attendants there that day, but he definitely stood out from the pack. His name was Larry. He was about 6'2" and much to my surprise, had long dreadlocks down his back (I would have expected an "achy, breaky" mullet). He lacked some teeth, and also sported a "Duck Dynasty" beard, years before it was cool. He also had quite the accent. When he walked up to my truck and started cleaning my windshield, making polite small talk, I kinda just stood there feeling pretty smart in retrospect, until he walked to the front of my truck. He reached for the grill and plucked out a dead insect. He held it out for me to see, and said, "This is a drone bee," and then began telling me in great detail about its anatomical makeup. At this point, I kinda zoned out and berated myself for assuming he was an idiot—I mean, look at him going on and on about the bee! I felt like such a jerk when I snapped back…

I said, "Where'd you learn all that?"

And he replied, "Texas State Penitentiary."

unrealistic

I made the mistake of asking what he did. Turns out, he killed his 8th grade guidance counselor. I was rather shocked, but tried to retain my composure as he reassured me he was completely rehabilitated. The only other "brush with the law" he's had was that time when he punched a stock boy at the Piggly Wiggly because they were out of turkey bacon. I gave him the benefit of the doubt as he finished cleaning my windshield. As we continued our small talk, he asked me if we had a lot of snakes in Arizona. I told him we had something of an infestation, and he replied by saying he had an answer to that problem. All I had to do was give him ten minutes to go home and get it. Because of my paralyzing fear of snakes, and my better judgment impaired by curiosity, I agreed to wait for him. When he returned, he was carrying a small cat carrier. He set it down and cautiously opened it. He started reaching inside, trying to grab whatever was in there. When it finally emerged, it was the world's ugliest dog. The poor little thing, just a bit bigger than a Chihuahua, had almost as bad of a haircut as its

poorly described

owner and had scars and bite marks all over it. It kinda reminded me of a combination between a hairless cat and a Tasmanian devil. He held it up by the scruff of its neck and said,

"This right here, this little sucker's a snake killing machine." At this point, I'm equal parts terrified and intrigued, so I thought, "Let's see what he's got."

So Larry takes the little mutant over to a tree and just throws him up into it. The little dog climbed like a squirrel up into the branches and disappeared into the thick leaves. You could see the branches rustling around, but not the dog. All of a sudden, I heard it start growling

> ### LOOK HERE
>
> Have you ever considered adopting a pet or volunteering at an animal shelter? To get involved with animal welfare in San Luis Obispo, visit either the Woods Humane Society:
>
> **http://www.woodshumanesociety.org/volunteers/**
>
> or, the SLO County Animal Services:
>
> **http://www.slocounty.ca.gov/AServ.htm**

and barking like a berserk war machine and leaves were falling out of the tree from the branch shaking, when out of nowhere, a dead snake fell from the tree. The crazy little bastard darn near gnawed its head off. I was totally impressed, *[hard to relate]* and despite its hideous exterior, I wanted one. Lucky for me, one just had puppies. Because of his past indiscretions, I decided, instead of going back to Larry's house, I would wait at the truck stop while he went to get the puppies. He brought them in a big bucket and while he proudly showed off each one, I tried to pick out the cutest one, and to my surprise found one that was actually pretty cute. (I reckon the other one just got bitten in the face too many times.) As soon as I made my pick, I looked into his eyes and knew he was born to be named Kevin Kerby Houghs. To this day, I have no ideas where that name came from, but it definitely suited him.

He sat on my lap the whole drive home and when he was grown, made it his mission to kill every snake in a ten mile radius of our house, much to my satisfaction. Years have gone by now but Keven Kerby Houghs continues his reign of terror around the ranch. One day, someone asked me what kind of dog he was, and I realized I had no idea. I dug through the file cabinet to find Larry's number, and dialed him up. *[Jumps quickly to present]*

When he answered, I said, "Hey, I bought one of those crazy snake-killing puppies from you a few years ago, and I forgot to ask. What do you call those things?"

And he replied, in his deep-southern drawl, "A Louisiana Tree Dog."

Alexa Batta is an Environmental Earth Sciences major.

CONSIDER THIS

- Batta establishes a unique tone in this essay. How would you describe the tone? Does Batta break any of the "rules" about writing (such as using slang) that you have been taught to follow?

- Does Batta "show" you her experience, or does she do more "telling"? Can you identify moments when detailed description drives her narrative forward?

Exploring Significant Moments

Braids of Glory

Julian Gordon

At the tender age of 7, I was a naïve boy. Trotting around the sandy deserts of Arizona, I believed that I was kind of the cosmos—that if I were to walk into Arizona's non-existent ocean, the hissing waves would pardon themselves and skirt around me so as not to tarnish my newly-acquired and ever-so-fashionable light-up Sketchers; it was my world, and I was merely allowing everyone to walk among its face. This particular mindset that reigned over my psyche acted as a catalyst for its own demise.

The rural, bleak Arizonian town of Three Points, set on the outskirts of Tucson, was the epitome of the middle of nowhere. In towns like this, the sudden whirring as the air conditioner kicked into gear was about as thrilling as the day got. Outside, all one could see were pathetic excuses of shrubs peppering the harsh, tanned dirt and grey cacti sporadically cluster in abundance, receding all the way to the hazy, blue-violet mountains in the distance. This exorbitant amount of open space permitted my mother to fulfill her childhood fantasy of owning horses. After we had settled into our home, she quickly had a corral installed behind our attempt at a garden and occupied it with three horses: a white Arabian sprinkled with grey spots, a tall, magnificent brown and white paint, and a very small, middle-aged bay mutt named Pippin. With Pippin's minute size, she technically was considered a pony, and therefore was the perfect height to accommodate three young children: my two sisters and myself.

A separate arena was erected on the edge of our property. Amidst a sea of dead, graying shrubs and twigs, a narrow, hardly distinguishable trail was cleared, snaking its way through the debris to the entrance of the coral.

One evening, as the sun began to dip below the rocky peaks for the faraway mountains, painting the sky with radiant hues of orange and a fiery pink, we lead Pippin into the arena for some grooming. She spent the first few minutes running laps along the barred fence, delighted as the wind caressed her brilliant mahogany fur, her long mane and tail waving majestically with each gallop. Once her energy was spent, and she calmed, my parents began picking her shoes clean and brushing her mane while my sisters and I took turns braiding her tail.

LOOK HERE

Check out these famous quotes about the benefits of laughter:

http://www.goodreads.com/quotes/tag/laugh

I, being a seven-year-old boy, hadn't the faintest clue how to braid. I was holding the tail in separate chunks twisting each one and occasionally crossing two, hoping I would figure it out along the way. In my state of pure concentration, I had become oblivious to a very crucial detail that could have saved me from the horror that was about to transpire. Not only had Pippin lifted her tail high, but just as well, my whole family had backed off for precautionary measures. They felt no need to warn me—perhaps they thought this travesty would amuse their sick minds. I continued aimlessly trying to understand the mechanics of a braid when suddenly, I was hit full in the face by the most rancid, unpleasant gust of wind, the likes of which no existing words can accurately portray. It was like nothing I had ever or henceforth experienced: an odor from the deepest bowels of Hell—an unequalled putridity that could only have been created by the wrath of Satan himself. It is something I wouldn't wish upon the worst of my hypothetical enemies. It seemed enough to rust the wire frames on my glasses, singe the eyebrows right off my face, and I cannot be certain, but I would be willing to bet that nearby foliage wilted upon contact with this stench. No living creature was designed to withstand such assault. My sense of smell had been violated to an almost unsalvageable degree. I could hear the relentless cackling coming from my audience, and being so young, my reaction to anything the slightest bit traumatic was to simply cry, so cry I did. As tears endlessly flowed down my cheeks, clearing paths in the dust that had settled on my skin, and sputtering gasps broke between wails, my mother guided me back into the house, stifling back her own laughter, and proceeded to clean me off until my sobbing subsided while everyone else took Pippin back to the corral for the night.

As trivial as this anecdote may seem, it did in fact change the way I perceived the world. I no longer ignored the occurrences around me. I no longer assumed that people would readapt themselves in my favor, but rather that I needed to meet them halfway. It taught me to be observant—to have what my father calls "10-direction eyes." At the time, this was a horrific and scarring experience and not the in the slightest way amusing; but I can now look back on it and laugh at my naivety; and any time I slip up and discover I have been heedless of something important, I am reminded of just what can happen when one is not constantly vigilant, all thanks to the simple, ordinary bodily function of a horse.

Julian Gordon is an Art major.

CONSIDER THIS

- Writing with humor isn't easy, but this essay is FUNNY! See if you can pinpoint the rhetorical choices the writer makes in order to tickle his audience's funny bone.

- How does the author's use of imagery enhance his message? Which images stand out most to you and why?

Heavenly View

Chris Leclair

Reflective Memo: *I loved writing this essay. My mind was given FULL freedom to formulate a structure for probably the first time in an English essay. As a first-quarter freshman, the topic was exciting and allowed me to expand my horizons—little did I know how literally this phrase would apply. I have always loved to explore the creative, descriptive part of my mind. Getting up early to hike the P set up for both a great experience and for my mind to be active and creative. Even still, I remember how difficult it was to start writing this essay. My head was spinning with ideas. I needed to convert the pieces in my head to a written puzzle. My essay took off when I started to write my ideas on paper—ALL of them—drawing connections and constructing a purposeful order. The hardest part in the writing process was starting without having a formulaic pattern to follow, but by winding down all my ideas, I was able to overcome this roadblock.*

Ultimately, this essay is a treasure of mine from my freshmen year of college and my introduction to San Luis Obispo. I hiked the P for the second time only a few days ago and I loved reminiscing on one of my first experiences: hiking the P for this essay. With summer quickly approaching, I was amazed at how quickly time has flown. What a year and what a view!

I stood panting deeply; the dry, airy taste of the raw terrain rolled around on my tongue. A short, safe distance away from my two friends and I, fully exposed on the barren hillside, two male deer were in a standoff. In late September, around the beginning of autumn, the buck undergoes an annual hormonal change known as rut, causing them to become more aggressive toward one another (Gee). The focus of each was driven onto the other and, simultaneously, their antlers clashed. Neither gained any ground on the other, and in fact, remained stationary. However, they repeated this maneuver several more times before noticing my presence and uniformly averting their gaze to me. My companions of the early morning and I exchanged stares and, without too much delay, returned to our respective objectives—the male deer continued butting heads and I proceeded to beat up the slope to the top of the hill.

I wondered why the deer continuously performed a seemingly pointless action. They remained fixated on each other and battled relentlessly, radiating the highest level of determination, though the activity yielded no apparent reward for either. As I observed their activity more, I could feel antlers

> **LOOK HERE**
>
> To see the rutting season in action, check out this video:
>
> **https://www.youtube.com/watch?v=vWvyIfcM_PA**

growing above my ears; I can, unfortunately, closely relate to the bucks in rut. I find myself intently focused on butting heads with the complications of my daily routine and toilsome aspects of my life in hopes of eventually gaining some ground, something to hold onto that represents reward for my efforts. However, I am inevitably caught in a perpetual cycle of distorted motivation. I seem to always be looking straight ahead—rarely around, up, or down from a hilltop beneath the heavens.

The hilltop above the "P," as identified by the Cal Poly students, raised me upward, out of my familiar mindset, into a new perspective evoked by the sensation that I was scanning the earth from a platform among the heavens. I sat perched on a rock, bearing witness to the breathtaking view from the peak of the hill, head swiveling at the majesty of my surroundings. The silence unchained my mind, and I began to drift into a rare state of aimless reflection. I cringed when I was interrupted.

"Lane Kiffin got fired," commented my friend Adam, checking his phone while sitting beside me at the top of the hill, "It's about time." In the voids in his daily life, Adam usually chooses to scroll through ESPN sports news or social media. Often, I no longer notice, as this practice fits the norm for both Adam and the vast majority of his peers. This morning, however, I noticed how out of place his phone was—how distinct his perspective was from my own.

"Yeah, good," I responded blandly. I was unable to muster any more commentary. I didn't want to waste my time on the hill by averting my focus. I didn't want to hear about the long-standing perils of the USC football program over the gentle whisper of the morning wind, hushing the earth as to quiet an anticipating audience for the spectacular entrance of the sun.

Adam does, I suppose, deserve some applause for his accomplishment of reaching the top of the hill. Our trip took place brutally early on a Sunday morning, and I am still surprised he joined me on the hike at all. Most of our fellow students would not be up for hours yet. Once we arrived on the Cal Poly campus a few weeks ago, we vowed to hike at sunrise the hill behind our dorms with the monstrous "P" etched in the face. So, we were motivated to visit one of our "sights to see" on campus and completed the hike. Conversely, our friend Yvette placed herself in her own distinct category. She too had gathered the audacity to rise at an inhumane hour, particularly for a Sunday. Nevertheless, immediately as the three of us reached the "P," located approximately halfway up the slope on the southeastern side of

LOOK HERE

To learn more about the "Poly P," check out this article by *Mustang News*:

http://mustangnews.net/poly-p-101-part-2/

the Cal Poly campus, Yvette exhaled, "Alright. You guys have fun, I'll be right here." With that, she thrust her hands deep into her sweatshirt and anchored her feet into the slope beside the "P," leaving half the mountain unclimbed.

Though my friends and I were all on the same terrain and below the same sky, we apparently chose to appreciate the morning in our respective ways. Adam and Yvette seemed to behold the morning with less grandeur than I—I was consumed and found myself caught in trance. More than the mere inhabitants, the entire valley that encompassed the campus of Cal Poly was asleep. From the very heart of this valley, the campus bell rang out, melodically yet forcefully, piercing my ears with each note, hypnotizing me, and plunging me into the art of observation. With each leisurely, powerful breath, my antlers subsided.

I saw the world, currently dim and lethargic, being painted into color gradually, prudently, gracefully by the Divine Artist, performing the same miracle as every day before. An incredibly subtle, intensifying glow off the jagged horizon erased the moon, a mere ghostly, arced sliver left behind by the fading night. The sun laid out rims of color shades around the horizon to glorify its dominant, assertive entrance into the sky. A profound blue-violet held up a thick shade of its complimentary color, orange, paired together only to be merged flawlessly by a thin seam of hot pink. The orange bled a soft yellow into the fullness of the sky.

Soon, the rocky tip of Bishop's Peak across the valley was the only patch of land marked by the sun, illuminated in golden brilliance. The sun broke the horizon from behind me, and the line of light gradually slid down the faces of Bishop's Peak and Madonna Mountain. Light glided closer to the valley and passively invaded, swooping down to fill San Luis Obispo with the colors of day that its inhabitants so enjoy. Warmth struck my back. And at that moment, I felt the overwhelming

sensation of my own body being painted with color by the sun—the sun that returned to paint the world today as it had done every day before since the beginning of God's creation. I remembered and reflected:

"In the beginning God created the heavens and the earth" (Genesis 1:1). He sits on His throne in the heavens, gazing down, extending His right hand to earth and His prized creation—me. And as I waited for the sun to creep over the horizon, I remembered the simplest facets of my being.

While I sat atop the peak, I realized that, as I propel myself through the ordinary days, my days turn to weeks, weeks to years, and years to memories. My perspective is powerful. Should I find myself lost in the midst of my struggles, focus forward and antlers drawn, the same sun will rise and start a new day, a refreshing beginning. I must reserve time to examine myself, rejuvenate my ambition for personal improvement, connect with my psyche, and recharge my inner peace. When I remove myself from the grind and sit among a blanket of transforming sky, perched up high looking down, the world becomes so simple and slow, placid and beautiful.

Adam and I trotted back down the hill to the "P" and met Yvette, still anchored in the same place. She looked at us, slightly annoyed, and asked, "Were you guys stuck up there or something?" "I wish," I muttered to myself, grateful for my unique opportunity. The three of us continued our descent into campus as the sun crawled higher into the sky. From the spot where I watched the deer battle earlier, I paused to scan the slope. The bucks had moved on long ago.

Chris Leclair is an Environmental Engineering major.

Works Cited

Gee, Ken. "In a Rut—Breeding Season Behaviors in Deer." *The Samuel Roberts Noble Foundation*. N.p., Nov. 2008. Web. 08 Oct. 2013.

Genesis. The NIV / King James Version: New International Version. Grand Rapids, MI: Zondervan Bible, 1985. Print.

CONSIDER THIS

- Why does Leclair frame his story with the anecdote about bucks during rutting season? Note every moment the author alludes to the bucks. How do the rutting bucks function as an extended metaphor?

- Leclair uses some effective and vivid descriptive language in this paper. Identify your favorite phrase or even word choices—what do these elements add to the paper's overall purpose and focus?

Not My Clay Doll

Kiana Chan

Reflective Memo: *This essay represents a discovery of myself through writing. It was a difficult process because it required me to critically think about myself in ways that I never have before. I am proud of the descriptive, anecdotal components of the essay that I feel describe my writing style and my experiences, capturing their depth and significance. After several revisions, I am happy about my final product because I believe that it demonstrates my improvement in writing over the course of the quarter.*

I plunged my pen-marked and glittery hands into the bag of cool, earthy clay and began sculpting the body of a girl. I started with her arms, legs and neck. Then, I grabbed a sculpting tool—like one that a dentist would use to scrape plaque off my teeth. Gradually, I dug the fine tip of the needle into her face, drawing her delicate facial features. Brown eyes with a black dot hidden beneath the iris, a nose that wrinkled when she smiled, and a short black hair bob with blunt bangs. After blending colors

> **LOOK HERE**
>
> To get another perspective on identity and race, check out this spoken word poem, "Ambiguous":
> **https://www.youtube.com/watch?v=o-nS8wgQNRk**

and final touches to my clay avatar, I cautiously, but proudly tiptoed across the classroom and set it on the table filled with the menagerie of my classmates' sculptures. All of the figures "wore" different colors for clothes, but I noticed that I was the only one in my class who used the color black for hair and tan for my face. What looked like a munchkin-sized, yet comparable representation of my outward appearance now looked awkwardly out of place amongst my class of mostly light skinned, light hair, and light eyed first-grade classmates. Although I felt out of place during school, once the school bells rang at 3:05 p.m., I would run out to the front of the school eagerly waiting for my dad's green Toyota Tundra. With my parents, I felt a sense of comfort knowing that I could be myself because they understood me. Maybe deep inside, I knew I was just like them.

"What are you?" This question makes me shrink a little bit inside. I think to myself; I am a person. I am a girl. I am a New Yorker. I am a Californian. The list goes on. I am Chinese. I am American. I am Kiana Chan. When I was younger, I usually grabbed the answer that I knew they were looking for: my ethnic background. "I am Chinese." But as I got older, I wanted to challenge

the uneducated question that spewed from their mouths and the stereotypes that accompanied and misrepresented Chinese identity. Sometimes, I would tell them, "I am American." But that answer was never enough for my classmates or complete strangers who asked. Because of my outward Asian appearance, they would not be satisfied with my reply and would persist with the micro-aggressive comment: "But what are you really?" As a child, I didn't know how to respond. I didn't understand the complexity of ethnic identity—and certainly neither did those who asked me. But now, I know that it's not my ethnic heritage that has shaped me. It has been the influences of my parents.

I am 5'5", and my long black hair falls over my shoulders like a mop. I awkwardly smile when I am nervous, and my cheeks turn bright red when I am embarrassed, caught off guard, or flattered. I enjoy wearing colorful, vibrant fabrics to represent my bright personality. I am 18-years-old, but I have the high-pitched voice of a child. When I stride, I swing one arm instead of two. I say hi to strangers. However, *I am* more than me. I am an individual embracing and struggling with what it means to be Chinese-American. After moving from southern Florida to the Bay Area, California when I was eight years old, I was shocked to be a part of a large population of Asian-Americans who, like me, all had black hair and brown eyes. And although we all have some

Figure 1: Winter break in Cabo, Mexico. 2013.

intersecting experiences by sharing a common heritage, this identity has a distinct meaning to each one of us. When I was younger, my ethnic identity automatically made me unique from my peers. I believed that I was completely different from my parents. I felt that I had nothing in common with them. However, as have become more independent and mature, I realize that their experiences and personalities have shaped who I am.

As a Chinese-American, I do not have a particular loyalty to either of these cultures. At home, Chinese culture is what our family makes of it. "Chi fan le! Yo, it's dinner time!" I hear my dad's attempt to speak Mandarin in his New York accent; his voice is loud like a fire alarm reverberating inside the house. His call rings with the cling clang of dishes, sizzling of stir-fried vegetables, and the mechanical song of our robot-like Zojirushi rice cooker. At home, we throw in Cantonese and Mandarin phrases here and there. We love the diverse dishes of Chinese cuisine. We remove shoes upon entering the house. I am Chinese American in every sense of the word—a mix of cultures that is unique to my family.

The lively characteristics of my parents developed from their upbringing in the fast-paced and boisterous New York City, which built a distinct foundation for the rest of my family. Loud and dynamic, they stood out amongst the quaint stillness of Pleasant Hill, California, our home for 13 years. My mother and father are what some would call, "polar opposites." Growing up, my dad told me stories about having his lunch money stolen in the schoolyard and pretending to only speak English so he could escape the Chinatown gang recruiters, getting into street fights on Mott Street after school with his classmates: Lemon Head, Monkey, Mongol, Bike Mike, and Toast. I grew up listening and laughing to his hilarious, interesting stories; but deep inside, I understood that it was not just fun and games for my dad: it was rough to live in the Lower East Side of Manhattan in the 1960s. My dad is strong and tall, arms and chest completely covered with symbolic tattoos representing our family; my mother's zodiac animal, the elegant and ferocious tiger roams through a bamboo forest. The Buddhist Goddess of Guan Yin sits on the right side of his chest, surrounded by intricate black clouds. My Chinese name, along with my younger brother's and older sister's, are imprinted on his arm. Despite his solid build, he throws tantrums when there is any food left in the sink after a meal and never takes "No" as an answer. My father is big and muscular, but I can't help but see him as a loving, extra-large sized baby who likes designer hair products and shops at J-Crew. He cleans and he cooks. He likes to buy nice things. He is a baby in a grown man's body.

Figure 2: My mother and father by the beach in Cabo, Mexico.

Although he grew up with very little money, his parents raised him like a prince within the walls of their New York City government-owned apartment. His mother laboriously peeled the delicate skins off of grapes for him to eat, and his father, a cook during World War II in Germany, fed him steak dinners. His parents showed their love for him through food. My parents had very different ways of displaying their affection for my siblings and me. While my mother would rather take us on long vacations to tropical, third world countries, my father preferred to show his love toward his children through the random toys, clothes, or gadgets that he bought for us. Thrifty like my mother, I would often decline his bribes to buy me sequined Betsey Johnson dresses or Swarovski crystal necklaces. This frustrated him because he didn't understand why his daughter would reject such nice gifts, a privilege that he never had as a child. He would often warn me with an urgent undertone in his voice, "Kiana, I'm serious, don't let mom get into your head. God dammit, buy whatever you want!" Although I appreciate my father's intentions, I agree more with my mother: life experiences are more valuable than material things. With two thousand dollars, we would rather buy round-trip airline tickets to Nicaragua than have a spring edition Marc Jacobs purse. It was hard for my father to accept the fact that we were different in our views towards material goods versus travel experiences.

Unlike my dad who obtains satisfaction from material goods, my mother lives for experiences. A luscious mane of hair, which she dyes with henna to disguise the aging grey, shimmers bright red in the sunlight. Although she was born when gas only cost fifty cents a gallon and when milkmen made the neighborhood milk deliveries, like Hebe, she has kept her youth and is often mistaken for one of her daughters from behind. She is free spirited and fun, yet assertive; she is unafraid to speak up if she disagrees with anything. Extremely extroverted, she befriends strangers in the park and on the New York City Subway. Filled with wanderlust, she dropped out of college during her second year, and against her mother's will, she left everyone she knew and bought a one-way ticket to Greece. She traveled across Europe with no plan, no place to stay, and minimal cash. Undefined by the precepts of a conventional mother, she is daring and ambitious, haphazard and carefree. A vacation with my mom includes volunteering on a pineapple farm in the tropical heat of Costa Rica, disguising malaria pills in Guyabano smoothies, and battling oversized mosquitoes with homemade vinegar bug spray.

Through the memorable vacations with my mother, I learned the extent her impetuous behavior, and also how similar I was to her and my father. During a vacation with just my older sister, Kaila, younger brother, Lucien, and mom, we stood hesitantly at the edge of the dock by Lake Atitlan, a vast, volcanic lake in the highlands of Guatemala. I saw my mother talking with a stranger in her nearly fluent Spanish. "Cuanto cuesta? How much?" she asked. Small in stature, with sun stained skin like leather, the man wore a disintegrating straw cowboy hat. He stood balanced on the edge of a deteriorating, sun-bleached rowboat tied loosely to the dock with a twine string. His mouth shaped into an algal grimacing smile and I could see his golden canine tooth glisten in the sunlight. My mother stepped onto the poorly crafted chunk of wood that sunk halfway under the weight of her body. Water crawled into the makeshift boat while she struggled to find her balance. Kaila, Lucien, and I stood wide-eyed with disbelief while we waited for our mom to barter our fate away with the ferryman from Hades. "Come on guys! Let's take this cute boat across the lake!" she persisted. I looked at Lucien, only seven at the time. In that moment, he wore his stubborn face with his pursed lips and wrinkled eyebrows, and Kaila, who was twelve, looked like she had just seen our grandmother's ghost. "Mom, no way!" I declared. I pointed towards the vast body of water, blanketed with pumice stones. After stubbornly remaining in the boat, she realized that she was outnumbered. Arms crossed in a teenage-like reluctance, she finally gave in. "Fine. Let's just be boring and walk around the lake instead." At only ten years old, I had to be persistent and assertive with my mom because she was just *too* easygoing. Completely oblivious to the danger of the situation, she was willing to risk losing our passports in the depths of the lake, and then what would we do in Guatemala for a month with no clothes, no malaria pills and no cash? Or what if we drowned? I felt like an ambassador to my siblings, protecting their lives from my adventure-craving mother. In that moment, I felt like my dad. When it came to potentially dangerous situations, my dad and I become very uptight and anxious. Our impatience and apprehension would not be cured until we resolved the situation. My mother always tells us both to "take a chill pill" in attempt to heal our uneasiness.

Growing up, I felt like the dominating personalities of my parents suppressed the development of my own character. Throughout my childhood, I was convinced that I was nothing like my parents. Preoccupied with trying to define what my ethnic identity means to me and who I am, I often lost sight of what was right in front of me. Just like my mom, I am spontaneous, adventurous, and extroverted. I thrive when challenges come my way, and I take the opportunities that will help me develop as a person. I am daring just like my mom. I dare to flee the country and leave all of my ties behind, just like my mother did in the midst of her college years, because I yearn for changes in my life. To travel the world by myself is a dream that I've had ever since I was young, but this dream did not just stem from my imagination. I live vicariously through my mom's experiences traveling across rural Germany in a burnt orange 1980s Volkswagen van, Salsa dancing in Cuba with her Spanish teachers, climbing snow-capped mountains in China. Through her, I have fallen in love with places that I have never been to. I am full of wanderlust like my mom; we believe that escape will cure our discontent. I have the desire to explore different countries not only to immerse myself in new cultures and languages, but also to discover who I am in different places, contexts and with different people. Although I am still discovering who I am, one thing I know for sure is that my desire to travel is almost uncontrollable. It is so hard for me to live in the present when I have so many visions, images, and experiences that I need to pursue during the timeframe of my life. When I travel, I feel free from the suffocating pressure that society has ingrained in me to define my ethnic identity and how it has shaped who I am. When I travel, I can be whoever I want to be.

But I am also just like my father. We are perceptive and observant. When he goes to restaurants, he sits in the chair that faces the door paranoid that someone with a gun could come in and start shooting. He always types his emails in CAPS LOCK because he thinks that everything he has to say is urgent. Incredibly cautious and very superstitious, he relied on timeless clichés to teach me life lessons. The early bird catches the worm. Always look for an open door. You snooze you lose. Be the best of the best. Despite our obvious differences, the similarities between my father and me have helped me learn more about myself. Our passion for cooking and food is only one thing that brings us together; through his actions and his personality, I have discovered parts of myself that are just like him.

Figure 3: My parents and me at a night market in Costa Rica.

In just a few years, I can imagine myself exploring the canals of Amsterdam, biking along its cobblestone paths, passing bright pastel homes and coffee shops with nothing but my wanderlust, my passport, and my memories from home. Or maybe I'll be cocooned in a frayed hammock on a wooden balcony, watching the rain pour down into the deep green Costa Rican rainforest, lost in thought about the distant memories of my childhood while sipping a warm, foamy cappuccino. Memories of my childhood like that of my clay doll: the one with black hair and brown eyes and felt so out of place among all of the other dolls. Where did she go? Is she lost forever?

೧

This figure has been lost for years. What was once a representation of myself as a child, no longer has the same meaning. Through my search for my identity, I have learned that neither my appearance nor my ethnicity classifies *me*. In my future travels, I will carry pieces of both of my parents that will distinguish who *I am*. It will serve as a constant reminder that I am my mother's wanderlust. I am my father's practicality. I am truly their daughter.

Kiana Chan is a Nutrition major.

CONSIDER THIS

- Do you think the writer effectively analyzes the question, "Who or what are you?" Perhaps consider your own identity. Would it be difficult to come up with one phrase, or even a paragraph to encompass who you are? Why?

- This essay is an excellent segue into the profile sequence. Who is the writer profiling other than herself?

- Chan includes three images in her essay. What do these images add to the narrative?

How do texts communicate with their audiences?
How do they make meaning?
What tools do they use to persuade readers, viewers, and listeners?

To understand how a text communicates meaning, we first need to identify not only the text's intended audience, but also the rhetorical appeals (*ethos, pathos,* and *logos*) it uses to persuade that audience. Only then can we determine if the text's argument is truly persuasive. In other words, analysis moves beyond summary and delves into the inner workings of a text to understand *how* it expresses ideas. Indeed, learning how to critically read texts of all kinds—written, imagistic, aural—will be one of the most essential skills you learn in this course.

CONSIDER THIS

- On the next page, you will find a simple object that appears around downtown SLO. What meanings does this object convey? Use the questions to guide you.

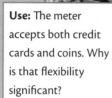

Use: The meter accepts both credit cards and coins. Why is that flexibility significant?

Location: This meter is located in front of the SLO mission. What is the significance of that location? Where are other meters located?

Audience: Who are the intended audiences for this meter? Does the meter rely on *ethos, pathos,* and/or *logos* to persuade?

Color: All of the meters are white, with a colorful "rainbow" label. What is the impact of that color scheme on a passerby?

Message: The meter reads, "Handouts don't help. Feed a meter, not an addiction." What problem is this meter trying to solve?

Kairos: Is there currently a problem with homelessness and panhandling in SLO? Why is NOW a good time to install these meters?

Context: How many meters are in SLO? Are they used in any other communities? Are they effective?

What Else: What other questions does this meter raise for you?

Make Change Count
Photograph by Brenda Helmbrecht

A Pep Talk

Kaitlyn Krautkramer

Reflective Memo: *This essay was perhaps the most challenging for me all quarter. I learned about analyzing rhetoric a little in high school, but this was the first time I had to break down all those devices and strategies and then write about them. I could pick out and identify many of the little things they used in the video, but it was hard for me to determine the importance of the choices and then write a whole essay about them.*

Part of my success in this essay was simply revising many drafts. I took them to my professor as well as the Writing and Rhetoric Center, and asked peers for advice. The final copy of this essay turned out quite different and cleaner than my first couple of drafts.

Since January 24th of this year, over twenty-nine million people have viewed the *YouTube* viral hit "A Pep Talk from Kid President to You." In this video, ten-year-old Robby Novak portrays a character known as "Kid President." Novak and his brother-in-law, Brad Montague, created Kid President about six months prior in an effort to encourage kids and adults alike to change the world for the better. They strongly believe that no matter an individual's age, they can do something to improve life for themselves and everyone around them. Although they never give us specifics on what exactly we should be doing, through Kid President the pair enthusiastically encourages us to be "less boring" and "more awesome." Novak and Montague weave an effective rhetorical net to draw us in and inspire us to reach the exciting goal of making the world a better place.

> **LOOK HERE**
>
> For information on Kid President click here:
>
> **http://kidpresident.com**
>
> Watch the "Pep Talk" here:
>
> **https://www.youtube.com/watch?v=l-gQLqv9f4o**

Throughout the video, Novak and Montague use lots of word repetition to emphasize how we all need to work together and start being more creative. For example, in the first thirty seconds or so, Kid President strings together words like "boring," "life," "game," and "team." Those terms plant themselves in our brains and make his main points a little easier to digest. He chose those words in particular to illustrate how he wants us to get up and go out into the world to help each other grow. It also accentuates the relationship between repeated words:

in this case with the goal of implying that we are "boring" unless we play on the same "team" in the "game" of "life."

Novak and Montague also use dancing as a symbol of their overarching goal of the project: to unleash people's innate "awesomeness." Dancing is a symbol of happiness and the freedom to create something extraordinary by using only one's body as a medium. A montage placed at the climax of the video features Kid President showing off his various dance moves, prefaced by encouragement to "give the world a reason to dance." By strategically placing this segment at the climax, the symbolic joy and freedom of dancing is emphasized. This symbol is used to inspire and motivate us, leading us to believe that we too can create something great by only using our own bodies and our innate creativity.

Kid President also brings up several cultural references, semi-seriously giving us advice on how to attain "more awesomeness." In one such case he quotes Robert Frost's "The Road Not Taken," joking that the road less travelled was painful and broke his pants. Novak and Montague are using a strategy here often used in humor, which is joking about or playing down something that we all admire, in this case Robert Frost's famous and admired poem. This allows them to use Frost's piece as an example while making it approachable and fun. After joking about the poem, Kid President tells us he wants to take the road "that leads to awesome," implying that it may be the one less traveled. Kid President goes on to purposefully misquote Journey and again jokingly wonders what would have happened if Michael Jordan had quit basketball in high school. In both cases, Novak and Montague use these humorously accessible references to give us examples of being better people and doing greater things. Since they are fairly popular cultural references, we are able to understand both the jokes and what they are really trying to hint at. Here, Novak and Montague are showing us who we could be and what we could accomplish in our quest to make the world better.

Finally, we will notice that Novak and Montague never actually state outright what they want us to do in terms of specific actions. Instead, they encourage us to do general things like get off our butts, persevere in our endeavors, and "create something that will make the world awesome." But beyond that, it is left to us as viewers to make of it what we want. This ambiguity allows us to interpret the message for ourselves, and therefore the video becomes relevant and applicable to virtually everybody who watches it. The pair believes that every person has a chance to make the world a better place. Their use of an intentional vagueness makes it possible to touch and inspire a wide range of people, all while using the same exact message. The reason why this is effective is that everybody has very different levels of commitment and involvement in making the world better. For example, say there is someone who lives a fairly average life but makes the not-so environmentally conscious decision of not recycling. A message about being green by recycling may be effective for that person, but not for another person who already recycles. For the person who is environmentally conscious, a message encouraging them to generally try to be more "green" opens up a lot of new possibilities. Not only would the broader message be effective in reaching the person who already recycles, but it would also have a beneficial effect on the person who is a little further behind environmentally. In this case, Kid President's message would be more of a general urging to go green rather than to just recycle.

If their twenty-nine million views are any indication, Novak and Montague prove to be very effective at getting through to their audience. Their clever and humorous way of encouraging us to be more awesome leaves the audience feeling inspired and motivated to fulfill their potential. No matter our situation in life, Novak and Montague remind us that we can all be better people. So now, as Kid President says, "create something that will make the world awesome."

Kaitlyn Krautkramer is an Animal Science major.

Works Cited

Montague, Brad, and Robby Novak. "A Pep Talk from Kid President to You." *YouTube*. YouTube, 24 Jan. 2013. Web. 29 Sept. 2013.

Montague, Brad, and Robby Novak. "Who We Are!" *KidPresident.com*. n.p., n.d. Web. 10 Oct. 2013.

CONSIDER THIS

- Try to plot the organizational structure of this essay—what is the governing idea of each paragraph? Is the organization effective or ineffective? Be sure to consider transitions and topic sentences.

- According to the writer, Kid President's "intentional vagueness" is a rhetorical choice that strengthens the commercial. Do you agree or disagree? Use a specific example from the commercial to support your argument.

- This writer does not discuss specifically Aristotle's three appeals and how they are employed in Kid President's video. After viewing the video, how would you add to this analysis by adding observations about the way Montague and Novak use those strategies to convince their audience to help make the world more awesome.

Analysis

Ethos, Pathos and *Logos* in
"We Need to Talk About an Injustice"

Fiona Cullen

A staggering number of children today are sitting in jail and will continue to do so for the rest of their lives. In 2005, for example, 2,484 children in the United States were serving life sentences without chance of parole. The United States is the only country that offers this sentence to children, and with the number of children being put away going up yearly, youth are increasingly being robbed of their chances to live freely (Agyepong). This issue, along with others pertaining to human rights and injustice within the American legal system, is one of the problems that Bryan Stevenson is working to address. As a public-interest lawyer and Executive Director of the Equal Justice Initiative (EJI), an organization fighting to stop unfair sentencing, exonerate innocent prisoners, and aid children being persecuted as adults, Stevenson is a prominent figure in his field and was asked to present at a TED Talk conference. In March

> **LOOK HERE**
>
> Read about and watch Stevenson's talk here:
>
> **http://www.ted.com/talks/bryan_stevenson_ we_need_to_talk_about_an_injustice**

of 2012, Stevenson gave a TED Talk titled "We Need to Talk About an Injustice" on some of the issues facing Americans today, such as children sentenced to life without parole, unfair sentencing, and racial discrimination present in today's justice system. Stevenson effectively uses ethos, pathos, and logos in his TED Talk in order to convince his audience of the racial prejudice and unjust practices present in today's justice system ("New to TED?").

Ethos, the rhetorical practice of convincing the audience of the author's credibility and ethics, is an essential aspect of Stevenson's speech ("Examples of Ethos, Pathos, and Logos"). During his speech, before even uttering a word, Stevenson stands on stage well dressed and well groomed, with confidence and a unique presence that does not go unnoticed by the audience. From the moment he walks on stage, Stevenson has begun to establish credibility with the audience that helps to convince them of his cause before he has even begun to speak. Independent of his physical appearance, Stevenson has academic and professional credibility as well. His title as Executive Director of the Equal Justice Initiative and his degrees from both Harvard Law School and the Harvard School of Government give him credibility as a professional and as an expert in his field ("New to TED?"). According to Mike Putnam of the University of Texas at Arlington, the audience

must trust that the speaker is "sufficiently knowledgeable to deal with the problem at hand," and in this case, Stevenson certainly is. Several times throughout his talk, Stevenson mentions his schooling and the number of years he has been a lawyer. These references to his vast experience and knowledge in his field allow him to establish a good rapport with the audience, which is essential to his persuasive strategy.

One of several anecdotes that Stevenson utilizes throughout his TED Talk is a story about his interaction with Rosa Parks and a couple of her friends, Johnnie Carr and Virginia Durr, who were also involved in the Civil Rights Movement. Stevenson reflects on how he was fortunate enough to be invited to listen in on several of their conversations over the years and discusses his involvement with EJI and aspirations to change the American legal system. Ethos is evident here in many ways. Parks, Carr and Durr are all very notable and recognizable figures in American history. The fact that Stevenson had their interest and support for his organization and plans for the future gives his cause credibility, and commands respect from the audience. In addition, his respectability as a speaker is influenced by this story because as someone who interacted with such prominent historical figures, he establishes respect for himself. On another level, TED as an organization is very well respected in today's academic community. To be a speaker at a TED Talk Convention is a highly coveted honor and a widely respected position within the academic community and beyond it. Stevenson recognizes this when he says: "One of the things that's emerged in my short time here is that TED has an identity. And you can actually say things here that have impacts around the world. And sometimes when it comes through TED, it has meaning and power that it doesn't have when it doesn't."

This idea of TED being a credible source in and of itself shows just how much its reputation comes into play in "We Need to Talk About an Injustice". Whether it be through the speaker himself, the view the audience has of the speaker, his interactions with others, or the medium in which the speech is presented to the audience, it is clear that Stevenson effectively applies ethos in his speech.

Similarly to his use of ethos, Stevenson uses pathos in his effort to persuade the audience. Pathos, which can be defined as a means used to persuade the audience by appealing to their emotions, is utilized emphatically by Stevenson to draw sympathy from the audience while talking about an emotional and impassioned topic. Empathy, a word derived from pathos, is at the heart of Stevenson's speech (Putnam). His goal is to get the audience to empathize with his cause so that they can join the fight to stop the injustice that is occurring in America. To begin his speech, Stevenson uses a story from his childhood about his grandmother and his relationship with her, stating:

> I grew up in a house that was the traditional African American home that was dominated by a matriarch, and that matriarch was my grandmother. She was tough, she was strong, she was powerful… She was the daughter of people who were actually enslaved.

By sharing his relationship with his grandmother, Stevenson gives the audience an opportunity to relate to him and become invested in his story on a personal level. In addition, by divulging that he and his grandmother are direct descendants of slaves, Americans who were treated in a horribly unjust manner, Stevenson reveals a reason he has become so impassioned to help those in similar situations today. There are a multitude of instances from our nation's history that many citizens are not proud of, and Stevenson uses some of these events to evoke empathy and guilt from the audience. Speaking again about the era of slavery and the decades that followed, Stevenson recalls the feelings of terror that were held back then:

> But for African Americans in this country, that was an era defined by terror. In many communities, people had to worry about being lynched. They had to worry about being bombed. It was the threat of terror that shaped their lives.

The terror that was seen in communities throughout the South decades ago is still seen in many communities around the world today. Simultaneously drawing connections between emotional events from history and emotional events that are taking place presently, Stevenson compels the audience to ponder how problems that were assumed to be relics of the past are still prominent modern issues.

Another aspect of pathos that Stevenson uses is guilt. Guilt is a powerful emotion and motivator, and he uses it to his advantage in his TED Talk. Again, Stevenson draws attention to problems and issues in America and delivers them in a manner that the audience can relate to. In one example, Stevenson combines facts and emotion to get his point across:

> The death penalty in America is defined by error. For every nine people who have been executed, we've actually identified one innocent person who's been exonerated and released from death row… I mean, it's fascinating. In aviation, we would never let people fly on airplanes if for every nine planes that took off one would crash. But somehow we can insulate ourselves from this problem. It's not our problem. It's not our burden. It's not our struggle.

A very select group of people can relate to being on death row, none of whom are Stevenson's direct audience in this case. However, many of his audience members can relate to being on an airplane and can connect on an emotional level with Stevenson's example.

After successfully getting the audience to relate to the issue at hand, Stevenson sends them on an emotional guilt trip: "It's not our problem. It's not our burden.

It's not our struggle." He uses these phrases to argue that despite those who may not think it is their responsibility to do something about it, it is in fact everyone's responsibility to stand up for injustice. Underlining this principle, Stevenson says, "The politics of fear and anger have made us believe that these are problems that are not our problems. We've been disconnected." In another example, he discusses the reaction that a certain audience member had to one of his talks that he gave in Germany regarding America's use of the death penalty.

> 'There's no way, with our history, we could ever engage in the systematic killing of human beings. It would be unconscionable for us to, in an intentional and deliberate way, set about executing people.' And I thought about that. What would it feel like to be living in a world where the nation state of Germany was executing people, especially if they were disproportionately Jewish? I couldn't bear it. It would be unconscionable. And yet, in this country, in the states of the Old South, we execute people …in the very states where there are buried in the ground the bodies of people who were lynched. And yet, there is this disconnect.

Again, Stevenson uses emotional events from history in order to get the audience to invest in his cause. Drawing parallels between our present day justice system, the crimes that took place during the Holocaust, and the era of slavery puts a heavy emotional weight on the audience. Connecting these issues on a global scale puts the issue into perspective against the ideals of other countries. By using these extremely powerful examples, Stevenson uses guilt and emotional investment to convince the audience.

The third part of Stevenson's persuasive strategy involves the use of logos: appealing to the audience by use of logic and reasoning ("Examples of Ethos, Pathos, and Logos"). Facts and statistics are one of the main tools that he uses to provide evidence for the injustices taking place in today's legal system. Stevenson states: "The United States now has the highest rate of incarceration in the world. We have seven million people on probation and parole" and goes on to include that, "this country is very different today than it was 40 years ago. In 1972, there were 300,000 people in jails and prisons. Today, there are 2.3 million." These are alarming statistics that definitely hold the attention of the audience. The drastic increase in the number of people our jails now held in comparison to the amount that were incarcerated just 40 years ago is frightening, and logically, a cause for concern. Following up this alarming statistic, Stevenson points out that "you're 11 times more likely to get the death penalty if the victim is white than if the victim is black, 22 times more likely to get it if the defendant is black and the victim is white." This fact doesn't reasonably make sense, unless you account for the racial bias and discrimination present in today's justice system. This statistic is backed up by Robert Staples in his article "White Power, Black Crime, And

Racial Politics," where he states, "[the] media's constant bombardment of images of black criminals and white victims creates and reinforces stereotypes in people's thinking." Clearly, racial bias and discrimination are a growing issue in this country, a fact that Stevenson expresses clearly during his TED Talk through the use of logos.

Using a wide variety of examples, personal anecdotes, and facts, Stevenson argues that certain aspects of the American justice system need to be changed for the better. Despite the fact that he does not address the other perspectives on some of his issues, he is still able to successfully communicate his points to the audience. Through his academic and professional success, he establishes an inherent credibility with the audience, effectively utilizing ethos in his presentation. He gives many personal stories and narratives in an effort to connect with the audience and get them to empathize with his cause. Lastly, using facts and statistics, Stevenson backs up his points with logical evidence of the crimes against human rights that are occurring in today's society. Using the rhetorical devices ethos, pathos, and logos to communicate his concerns for these issues in today's justice system, Stevenson gives an impassioned speech which is sure to resonate with audiences and empower them to take action against these problems.

Fiona Cullen is a Recreation, Parks, and Tourism Administration major.

Works Cited

Agyepong, Tera. "Children Left Behind Bars: Sullivan, Graham, And Juvenile Life Without Parole Sentences." *Journal of International Human Rights* 9.1 (2010): 83–102. *Academic Search Premier*. Web. 28 Oct. 2013.

"Examples of Ethos, Logos and Pathos." *Ethos, Pathos Logos Explanation and Examples*. n.p., n.d. Web. 05 Nov. 2013.

"New to TED? (11 Talks)." *New to TED?* TED, Mar. 2012. Web. 03 Nov. 2013.

Putnam, Mike. "SPCH 4302 Notes." *SPCH 4302 Notes*. University of Texas, Arlington Department of Communication, n.d. Web. 04 Nov. 2013.

Staples, Robert. "White Power, Black Crime, And Racial Politics." *Black Scholar* 41.4 (2011): 31–41. *Academic Search Premier*. Web. 29 Oct. 2013.

"Transcript for Bryan Stevenson: We Need to Talk about an Injustice." *Bryan Stevenson: We Need to Talk about an Injustice*. Dotsub, n.d. Web. 04 Nov. 2013.

CONSIDER THIS

- Cullen begins her analysis by offering a statistic about the number of children in correctional facilities in the United States. While this figure is compelling, how does it enhance her analysis of Stevenson's talk? That is, does Cullen's outside research compel you as a reader to pay attention to the analysis she presents on Stevenson's TED Talk? Why or why not?

- Words such as "guilt" and "manipulation" often hold negative connotations, but the writer here uses them to suggest that Stevenson succeeds at reaching his audience. Given the topic, do you think it's appropriate to affect the audience in such a way? Or, are there other words you can think of that might also point to the emotions Stevenson draws upon to successfully convince his audience that we need to talk about injustice?

Giving Thumbs Down to "Thumbs Up"

Carol Fuss

As one of the wealthiest countries in the world, the United States often experiences an obligation to aid lesser-developed countries through disaster relief programs and philanthropy. In fact, the average American household contribution to charity in 2011 was $2,213 ("Charitable Giving"). Widespread use of the Internet has made it even easier for Americans to get involved with charity through online donations and awareness promotions. With advancements in technology such as smartphones, tablets, and free Wi-Fi, Americans have taken to social media to promote awareness of their favorite causes. Joining a cause has become as simple as "liking" a page on Facebook. However, a recent advertising campaign has called the effectiveness of social media awareness into question. Crisis Relief Singapore's ad campaign, entitled "Liking Isn't Helping," utilizes pathos, logos, and ethos to implore viewers to step away from their keyboards and directly make a change in the world through volunteering.

One particular ad from the campaign displays a young girl standing thigh deep in dirty floodwater. Although the girl is front and center, the viewer's focus is also directed toward a group of hands surrounding the girl, giving her a "thumbs up" that resembles the "like" sign on Facebook. The ad offers an explanation of this gesture in a small message: "liking isn't helping." Another message, which reads, "Be a volunteer. Change a life," is displayed in the corner of the photo along with the logo and web address of the Crisis Relief Singapore organization. The ad is entirely black and white with small white text, which gives the photo a somber atmosphere.

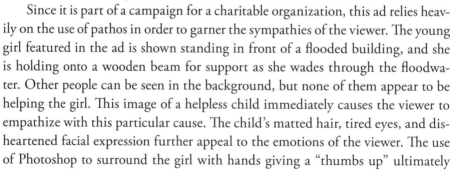

LOOK HERE

Check out the Crisis Relief Singapore ad campaign here:

http://www.featureshoot.com/2014/02/liking-isnt-helping/

Since it is part of a campaign for a charitable organization, this ad relies heavily on the use of pathos in order to garner the sympathies of the viewer. The young girl featured in the ad is shown standing in front of a flooded building, and she is holding onto a wooden beam for support as she wades through the floodwater. Other people can be seen in the background, but none of them appear to be helping the girl. This image of a helpless child immediately causes the viewer to empathize with this particular cause. The child's matted hair, tired eyes, and disheartened facial expression further appeal to the emotions of the viewer. The use of Photoshop to surround the girl with hands giving a "thumbs up" ultimately solidifies the ad's appeal to pathos. Although there are many hands surrounding the girl, not one of them is actually reaching out to help her. The girl herself is not reaching out to these hands either; instead, she is regarding them with a look of despair. This establishes a clear disconnect between a cause and the people who "like" the cause on Facebook.

In addition to tugging at the heartstrings of the reader, this ad utilizes the viewer's guilt in order to gain support. The fact that the hands in the photo are capable of helping the girl but are doing nothing to alleviate her struggle indicates that people are taking a lazy approach to philanthropy by offering intangible support through social media. The slogan also asserts that although supporting a cause via social media may make someone feel altruistic, simply "liking" a cause on Facebook does not help someone in need. This essentially puts the viewer in the place of one of the anonymous hands surrounding the helpless girl. Thus, the viewer feels inclined to help those affected by natural disaster by visiting Crisis Relief's website and volunteering as the ad suggests. Although the photo does not show a child directly seeking aid, the use of pathos to appeal to the sympathy and guilt of the viewer creates a subtler cry for help that is made even more effective in combination with the use of logos and ethos.

This advertisement's appeal to logos greatly enhances the emotional message that it conveys. The slogan, "liking isn't helping," uses a logical argument to persuade the reader that "liking" a charity or cause on social media does not constitute helping those in need. This idea is also established through the visual representation of "liking" that is displayed in the photo. The use of a literal interpretation of a logical argument is very effective because the reader is able to comprehend the main idea of the campaign without solely relying solely on the emotional appeal of the photo. Rather than employing pathos and logos in distinctly separate ways, the advertisement allows pathos and logos to work in conjunction to contribute to the overall appeal to ethos.

In this advertisement, ethos is used to gain the trust of the reader. The organization effectively reaches its audience by employing a modern reference as their main focus. Through the visual representation of "liking" something on Facebook, this ad demonstrates the ineffectiveness of social media awareness campaigns in a manner that is relatable to all Facebook users. This ad is especially geared toward younger audiences, such as teenagers and young adults, as they are the most frequent users of social media. Therefore, this audience is more inclined to trust the message of the ad because they are able to understand its context in modern society. The simplicity of the ad also contributes to its appeal to ethos. The ad utilizes minimal text and does not employ larger, flashy symbols that distract from its meaning. Additionally, the ad calls people to action (through the use of pathos) rather than simply asking for donations. This humble approach causes the reader to believe that Crisis Relief is a valid organization

that is truly dedicated to making a change in the lives of others. Consequently, viewers are more inclined to become involved with the organization and make a change themselves.

Given the strong pathos, logos, and ethos rhetorical appeals of this ad, it is no surprise that it won a prestigious Gold Lion award at the Cannes Lions International Festival of Creativity this year ("Liking Isn't Helping"). The ad evokes the sympathy of its audience while presenting a logical and humble argument in order to persuade people to more actively participate in crisis relief efforts. The use of modern references to social media provides a contrast between those who are left helpless in the face of a natural disaster and those who are comfortable to offer minimal support from the comfort of a desk chair. Through these techniques, Crisis Relief Singapore attempts to reach an audience that is capable of extending benevolence to those in need.

Carol Fuss is a Business Administration major.

Works Cited

"Charitable Giving Statistics." *nptrust.org.* National Philanthropic Trust, 2013. Web. 11 Nov. 2013.

"Liking Isn't Helping: Publicis Facebook Campaign For Crisis Relief Singapore Wins Top Award." *huffingpost.co.uk.* The Huffington Post, 26 June 2013. Web. 11 Nov. 2013.

CONSIDER THIS

- Writers are often advised to use third person when writing formal essays because doing so can create a balanced tone and avoids implicating one's readers. However, writers can consciously opt to incorporate sentences using first and second person to achieve a particular stylistic effect. How might this essay have changed had the author used "I," "you," or "we"?

- Fuss claims that this advertisement uses pathos, logos, and ethos to create a powerful message. Do audiences often find the rhetorical appeals working together in a balanced fashion? Or, based on your reading of this essay, does it seem that one of the appeals was more widely employed in the ad to reach its audience? Does that help or hinder the ad's effectiveness?

Chipotle: "Food with Integrity"

Emily Cheung

Reflective Memo: *For this assignment, I needed to pick a piece and rhetorically analyze it, so at first I simply Googled "rhetorical pieces." I got a lot of results of presidential speeches, and I even decided to analyze one. However, a page into my essay I realized that I really had no interest in analyzing that piece. Afterwards, I really gave myself time to think about something I wanted to write about and finally settled on analyzing a Chipotle video advertising their new game. I absolutely enjoyed every second of writing this essay, and I am so glad I changed my topic to something I was interested in. Choosing a topic you like really makes a huge difference when it comes to writing.*

In today's gluttonous and fast-paced society, we as consumers tend to overlook the quality and manufacturing methods of fast food. Since big corporations generally fulfill America's desire for instant gratification with their processed food, small farms that produce fresh wholesome food struggle to survive. That is, the cost of ingredients has gone down for corporations at the expense of a fresh, healthy meal. Despite this trend, the Mexican-food chain Chipotle abstains from such industrial techniques, promoting anti-factory farming through its powerful animated short called "The Scarecrow." This animation, which advertises their new app game, appeals to the consumers' sense of pathos and ethos to increase interest in healthful and sustainable food.

As the film opens, a melancholy scarecrow with expressive, obsidian eyes enters a smoky building, Crow Foods Incorporated. Fiona Apple's haunting rendition of the ballad "Pure Imagination" accompanies this animated short as the scarecrow begins his bleak day at work. While being dictated orders by a crow, the scarecrow witnesses the horrors and deceits of the food-processing factory behind closed doors. Through his eyes, the viewer experiences an array of disturbing scenes. Among these are a tube extruding a processed substance marked "100% Beef-ish," a robotic crow injecting an "all natural" chicken with a green fluid, and a trembling cow with fearful eyes confined inside a small metal cage.

LOOK HERE

Watch the Chipotle ad:

https://www.youtube.com/watch?v=lUtnas5ScSE

After a disheartening day at work, the scarecrow returns to his home and notices a bright red chili pepper in his garden. Struck with inspiration, he returns back to the city and uses his fresh vegetables to create his own restaurant. The short concludes with the scarecrow shooing away a crow and a banner falling down, which says, "cultivate a better world."

The film draws its viewers in on an emotional level through its ironic setting. The traditional depiction of a scarecrow keeping away crows has immediately been distorted: in this imaginary world, the crows are in charge of the scarecrows. This break from normality creates an ominous and uneasy mood. Because of this extreme reversal of roles, viewers expect the following events to be disturbing and bizarre as well. The mishaps that follow are in fact disturbing, but they are not bizarre—they accurately portray what goes on in our world. This unexpected insight on corporate practices highlights and portrays factory farming in a negative light, reminding us that even though these methods are common, we should not necessarily accept them heedlessly.

Another effective rhetorical technique implemented in this animated short is the personification of the scarecrow. The scarecrow's sullen facial expressions as he encounters the exploitation of the animals induce sympathy in the viewers. Every time the scarecrow takes a peek into the shady processes of the factory, the viewers see from his perspective. Because they are in his shoes due to his humanistic qualities, viewers are encouraged to empathize with the scarecrow and feel equally horrified by what they witness.

The crows also play a role in urging consumers towards healthier food choices. Considering crows are superstitiously associated with bad luck, they indicate misfortune as a result of poor food production methods. By extension, crows represent death, which indicates that these unhealthy practices are detrimental to our environment. The crows also have menacing red eyes. From this imagery, the crows are portrayed as villains and evoke ill feelings. Since the crows ultimately run the factory, they symbolize big corporations that use similar processing methods.

Now that the film has created an intense and mournful atmosphere, it brings forth a beacon of hope. The mood of the film noticeably changes when the scarecrow discovers a red chili pepper—Chipotle's logo. Compared to the dull and lifeless surrounding, the vibrant red colored vegetable looks extremely delectable and appealing. The skies brighten and even the morose ballad changes into a happier tune. This prominent change conveys that unlike typical corporations, Chipotle is healthier, natural, and ideal. The red pepper, as Chipotle's logo, reminds us about its real life business practices geared towards the health of both the consumer and the environment.

With over 1500 locations around the world, Chipotle can be considered a very successful food chain ("2012 Form 10-K"). Because of its success, Chipotle has a strong reputation in the food industry. Unlike most fast-food chains, Chipotle is believed to reject "almost every major technique on which the industry was built" (Times Wire). Rather than maximizing profits through cheap means of processed food, Chipotle claims to have food with integrity—"Chipotle's commitment to

changing traditional 'fast food' culture by serving customers the very best ingredients, all raised with respect for the animals, the environment and the farmers"
(FWI).

In the film, Crow Foods Incorporated's "100% beef-ish" product is evidently
not pure beef; this processed meat has other substances as well, hence the "ish"
on the food label. It is also revealed that the "all natural" chicken is not so natural after all; the chickens are injected with antibiotics. Moreover, all the animals
suffer harsh conditions, such as tight living spaces. However, Chipotle allegedly
does not conform to these methods. Because they prefer working with respect-
able family farms, Chipotle truly uses all natural meat from animals that are not
injected with antibiotics and are able to "display their natural tendencies" due to
better living conditions ("FWI Facts").

Chipotle's short film convinces us to reconsider our food choices. By continuously purchasing food from corporations that work with farm factories, we
are jeopardizing our environment and the quality of our food. As consumers, we
have the choice to follow the footsteps of the scarecrow by shooing away the crow.
The call for action to "cultivate a better world" is in our hands.

Emily Cheung is a Nutrition major.

Works Cited

Chipotle Mexican Grill. "The Scarecrow." *Youtube.* Youtube, 11 Sept. 2013. Web.
6 Oct. 2013. n.p. Chipotle Mexican Grill n.d. Web. 10 Oct. 2013.

"FWI Facts." *Chipotle.* n.p., n.d. Web. 6 Oct. 2013.

Times Wire. "Chipotle Chalks Up Success By Defying Fast-food Gospel."
SPTimes. Tampa Bay Times, 24 Nov. 2007. Web. 6 Oct .2013.

"2012 Form 10-K, Chipotle Mexican Grill, Inc." United States Securities and
Exchange Commission. 12 Feb. 2013. Web. 6. Oct. 2013.

CONSIDER THIS

- The writer uses descriptive language when summarizing the Chipotle film. How
  does her word choice enhance her analysis of this ad? What other writing strategies
  does she employ to provide readers with a vivid understanding of the film?

- At the end of the essay, the author draws information from Chipotle's website.
  Discuss the ways in which her analysis would have been different without that
  information.

What it Means to be "Vogue"

Hannah Mazet

"That is so vogue" is a phrase that has been used in the fashion industry for decades, but what is the allure in the word? Vogue is defined by *Merriam-Webster* as "something (such as a way of dressing or behaving) that is fashionable or popular in a particular time and place." So, naturally, the magazine *Vogue* is filled with all the things in life that glimmer, are "in the now," and, for most, are highly unattainable. It is a monthly compilation of trendy styling and dieting tips as well as jaw-dropping advertisements from designers such as Oscar de la Renta, Prada, Tiffany & Co., and Burberry. As you flip through the magazine page by page, you see one stunning model after the other, adorned in thousands of dollars of high-end clothing and accessories. Through advertisements, articles, and photographs, *Vogue* magazine embodies style and luxury at its utmost finest, while giving little attention to all that is simple and readily available in one's life. While elegance and appearance are highly valued in the fast-paced world we live in today, money and glamour should not define one's happiness, as *Vogue* magazine makes it out to be.

Vogue was founded in 1892 by Arthur Turnure, a New York society man, as a weekly publication in the U.S. (though now published monthly) in hopes of celebrating "the ceremonial side of life." In the words of Turnure, the "ceremonial side of life" he aimed to celebrate,

> ha[d] in the highest degree an aristocracy founded in reason and developed in natural order [...] The ceremonial side of life attract[ed] the sage as well as the debutante, men of affairs as well as the belle. It may be a dinner or it may be a ball, but whatever the function the magnetic welding force [was] the social idea. (qtd. in Smith)

As supported by Turnure's quote, the magazine was founded solely for the purpose of celebrating the highest level of aristocracy (the superior social class), with no intention of shedding light on the beauty of the simpler things in life. Nevertheless, since its founding, *Vogue* has become "the most influential fashion magazine in the world," reaching an outstanding 11.3 million people per month in print and averaging 1.6 million online viewers per month (Smith).

LOOK HERE

To experience *Vogue*'s "ceremonial side of life," check out the magazine's Instagram page: **http://instagram.com/voguemagazine**

As you open the first page of the Jessica Chastain December 2013 edition, what do you see? Matthew McConaughey and Scarlett Johansson, in a black and white image, posing gracefully for a Dolce & Gabbana advertisement for perfume. The photograph consumes both sides of the page, leaving you with no choice but to see the allure of the people and the product. You appreciate Johansson bundled up in McConaughey's arm, while his other arm is pointing out to the distance as though he's longing for something. Cleverly, where he is pointing, Dolce & Gabbana's advertisement gurus have placed bottles of their male and female fragrances, "The One," making it seem as though what this amazing-looking man is longing for is the perfume. The perfume bottles are the only part of the ad that is not in black and white. Instead, they are depicted in their original colors of a gold liquid in a clear glass bottle. The gold tint to the perfume adds to the warming effect of the idea that this perfume is "the one," just as Johansson does by radiating the feeling of love in her romantic black lace dress. In a significantly large font, the advertisers have written "Dolce & Gabbana the one" about four inches above the bottles. They wittily chose a grey font to mesh in with the black and white image, as not to take away from the focus of the page, the perfume. To top off the perfection of the ad, Johansson and McConaughey's celebrity vouch for the perfection of the perfume, leaving consumers craving the product. *Vogue* very cleverly chose this advertisement to be the first page in the edition, but why? First off, Johansson and McConaughey are very well known actors and are extremely beautiful individually, so when put together they make a pair of the highest elegance. Secondly, everyone and their sister knows Dolce & Gabbana, so the editors start the magazine by establishing that they know fashion and they know what is trending and craved today. This all builds on the idea that *Vogue* magazine is of superior style, class, and grandeur because these celebrities have all that embodies those ideals: fame, glamour, and style.

After countless pages of designers, advertisements, and photographs, you get to the small amounts of substance in the magazine: the beauty, travel, and dieting guides. In their "flash" section, *Vogue* included an article written about columnist Elisabeth TNT's adventures through the jungle in Borneo. She went on vacation to Borneo with her friend, Eva-Maria Shuman, to hike the island's highest peak, scuba dive in shark-infested waters, and explore the jungle. But for these two ladies, this was not a vacation to which they had become accustomed because the nature aspect was usually demure in their previous vacations. They had a packing list that entailed leach socks, mosquito nets, CamelBaks, and other items of the sort, none of which they were familiar—indicating to us as readers that these ladies are not the down and dirty type, but more of the Sunday garden party persuasion. So when they embarked on their excursion, it was no surprise that this "vacation" was an experience they had never encountered before. Elisabeth TNT explains, "Trekking sandals are the accessory of the moment, and a protein bar is as much a luxury as a dollop of caviar atop a baked potato from Paris' Kaspia" (Malle). She goes on to explain some of their adventures in more depth, but with each explanation she includes a follow-up sentence pointing to her high socioeconomic status. For example, "I do like a challenge—just ask my trainer,

Dmitri, at Bodyism in London," a highly coveted gym in the five star Bulgari Hotel in Knightsbridge. Elisabeth TNT later goes on to say after their very fun but "difficult" vacation, "Thankfully, there was a bit of pampering to come— at a pair of Shangri-La Resorts…[they] made sure we were fed, massaged, and snuggled into clean and crisp white linen sheets" (Malle). It is ironic that though Elisabeth TNT chose to go on vacation to an exotic, gorgeous island, much of her happiness did not come from hiking the highest peak, but from the spa at the end of the trip. Above the article the magazine's editors placed a large picture of the author posing on a rock in the middle of the jungle. Though dressed in the appropriate gear, she is leaning back in the photo and holding out a peace sign, making the picture as vogue as one can muster in hiking boots.

While the article was most likely written to shed light on a new and upcoming vacation destination and the luxurious hotels that are available on the island, this piece of work is a clear indicator of the demographic that *Vogue* aims to reach: women of age thirty to late forties who have money to spend and time for such opulent vacations. By including sentences that point to Elisabeth TNT's lifestyle, the readers, who also live a lush lifestyle, feel as though they can relate to her, making the vacation appeal to them as well. The issue that remains is that by including caviar remarks and other statements of that sort, Elizabeth TNT downplays the simple beauty of nature that could be experienced on this trip, reinforcing the idea that this magazine's sole purpose is to focus on all that is rich and extravagant in today's world.

At the end of the December 2013 issue of *Vogue*, there is a series of photographs of similar models wearing various clothing designers. In this particular piece, the series of photographs is called "The Silk Road," continuing the theme of adventure in the most glamorous mode possible, as photographed by Mario Testino, a well know Peruvian photographer. Testino included an introduction to the collection, "In Istanbul's collision of cultures, Kate Moss and actor Chiwetel Ejiofor meet. He radiates the luster of incandescent talent; she wears resort looks with the urbanity and refinement of the city itself." His photos capture the romance of the two in a variety

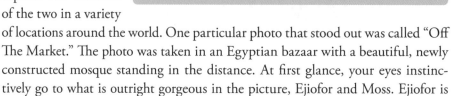

LOOK HERE

To see the slideshow of Testino's "The Silk Road" images, including the one of Ejiofor and Moss, go here:

http://www.vogue.com/magazine/article/kate-moss-and-chiwetel-ejiofor-in-resort-looks-in-istanbul/#1

of locations around the world. One particular photo that stood out was called "Off The Market." The photo was taken in an Egyptian bazaar with a beautiful, newly constructed mosque standing in the distance. At first glance, your eyes instinctively go to what is outright gorgeous in the picture, Ejiofor and Moss. Ejiofor is wearing a Prada suit with Moss, tightly clenched in his hand, wearing a Dior silk bodysuit and a Jason Wu linen skirt. The swanky couple walk together through the bazaar with such grace that they appear to be gliding through the scene, as if they were walking on clouds. Realistically, they are not gliding through the Egyptian bazaar, but the fact that they appear to be doing so gives them the essence of being angelic or of supreme beings. This perception all relates back to the idea that *Vogue* magazine's target audience since it was founded (and to date) want to see uncomfortably stunning people wearing the highest class of couture while participating in adventurous activities in seemingly attainable life circumstances.

Among Ejiofor and Moss, you see the people of the bazaar going about their day, from fathers and businessmen to grandmothers and children. This imagery brings a sense of reality to the image, as though this could be you traveling with your spouse in style. The backdrop of the scene is occupied by a tall and beautiful mosque, but the mosque is so easy to overlook due to Ejiofor and Moss's large presence. Reinforcing the couple's strong charisma and class is a Porsche that is conveniently parked in the middle of the bazaar. While having a Porsche in the middle of this town's center is unrealistic, it again gives the couple a sense of supremacy as though they have the right to park what and where they please. Additionally, throughout the image you see a repetition of gorgeous, vibrant red. In psychology, red is thought to be the most emotionally intense color; it can spark a fast heartbeat and bring the feeling of love (Johnson). Testino, knowing this much as an artist, purposefully used these red accents throughout the image to ignite the readers with a sense of intensity and maybe even love. Though the photo is as chic as chic gets, it pays no mind to the culture of the scene. Ejiofor and Moss are two overly gorgeous people, wearing seven thousand dollars in clothing, parading through a small town in Egypt. But instead of recognizing the culture, we are only able to focus on the high fashion.

This image defines what it means to be "vogue." The two models are on a vacation in another country, wearing superior clothing, and showing the village people that they are people of a higher boldness and class. That image is exactly what *Vogue* magazine wants people to see and aspire to. They do not want an image of a young Egyptian girl playing soccer with her friends in the street. They want their readers to see two perfect people, enjoying a lavish vacation, and presenting themselves with the utmost class. Likewise, that is what their demographic wants to see. *Vogue*'s readers want to see all the new trending high fashion, the new beauty products, and the details on the next best vacation destination, because for their older demographic that is the life they live.

In the midst of the solely materialistic point of view that *Vogue* magazine depicts, why have people been coming back for more for over a century? The answer to this question is two pronged. First, the portion of their demographic that can afford such designer clothing and extravagant vacations want a magazine that validates their high social standing and gives fashion advice, which for them is attainable. Second, today's culture is defined by beauty.

Analysis

As unfortunate as it is, our minds instinctively gravitate towards beauty and perfection just as Charles Darwin explained through his theory of natural selection. Therefore, even though a portion of *Vogue*'s demographic cannot afford the fashion in their magazine, they still read it because they aspire to be able to obtain such high beauty and style. For just those reasons, *Vogue* has been able to thrive for the past one hundred and twenty-one years, since its founding, ignoring the beauty of simplicity and narrowing in on the art of materialism.

Hannah Mazet is a Business Administration major.

Works Cited

Dolce & Gabbana. Advertisement. *Vogue* Conde Nast, Dec. 2013: 1–2. Print.

Johnson, David. "Color Psychology." *Infoplease*. Infoplease, n.d. Web. 03 Dec. 2013.

Malle, Chloe. "Elisabeth TNT Writes Her Own Jungle Book, Scaling the Heights of Borneo and Deep-Sea Diving in the South China Sea." *Vogue*. Conde Nast, Dec. 2013: 160–66. Web.

Smith, Emily E. "The Early Years of *Vogue* Magazine." *Acculturated*. n.p., 26 June 2013. Web. 01 Dec. 2013.

Testino, Mario. "Off The Market." 2013. Photograph. "The Silk Road: Kate Moss and Chiwetel Ejiofor in Urban Resort Looks." *Vogue*. Conde Nast, Dec. 2013. Web.

"*Vogue* (magazine)." *Wikipedia*. Wikimedia Foundation, 12 Apr. 2013. Web. 01 Dec. 2013.

CONSIDER THIS

- When analyzing the Dolce & Gabbana perfume advertisement, the writer uses the informal phrase, "everyone and their sister." Does the shift in tone hinder or enhance her ethos? Does this phrase help the writer connect with her audience, or is it distracting?

- Mazet does not hide her bias against the materialistic nature of *Vogue* magazine. How does the author's angle inform the three specific texts from the magazine that she chose to analyze?

- Mazet uses her analysis of *Vogue* to convey the belief that simplicity is perhaps more beautiful than materialism. Does Mazet provide sufficient evidence throughout her analysis to support this point of view? Do you agree or disagree with her position?

A Beautiful Failure

Lydia Kwong

Reflective Memo: *In this essay, I wanted to pick a focus that had many elements to choose from and really write about. The commercial I picked did not have too much or too little; as well, the commercial featured something that I enjoy watching: anime. Sure, it was not an actual anime feature, but it was close enough to it to make me want to write about it.*

It was hard work writing this essay, but it was also fun because I got to write about something I wanted. This commercial helped me go into depth because of all the details that it provided made it easy to get my ideas on paper. The biggest challenge I had was working the essay to make it clear and concise. I also struggled with passive voice. I was able to fix most of the errors and am proud of myself.

Flying seagulls chirping through the sunset sky made up of warm blue and orange tones begin this story. The scene switches to a glistening ocean where a boat starts to leave a port as a high school girl watches from afar. The next shot introduces tall buildings blurred into background while a high school boy crosses a bridge looking into the distance. Under the same sky, these two high school students (the girl, Miho, and the boy, Shouta) live different lives as they prepare for the Tokyo University college entrance exams. The music starts as they both physically move towards their common goal. Miho lives on a small island with no cram school (a Japanese tutoring program) to be found, and Shouta juggles a part time job on top of school. They both sign up for the same cram school, Z-Kai online. With the help of this cram school's correspondence courses, they take the entrance exam. The two unexpectedly cross each other's paths as they bump into each other on the day they find out whether or not they passed the test.

At first glance, this video does not look or sound like a commercial. However, it is a colorful and story-filled animated cartoon advertisement called, "Z-Kai: Crossroad." This Japanese commercial implicitly tells high school students about Z-Kai and how the program can help them get into a university without travelling to a designated place for help. Instead, students receive supplemental work from the company that they can complete whenever they have time to do so. The commercial shows that any high school student of any background can get into a college that he or she desires with the help of Z-Kai. Although this commercial appeals to its audience through emotions and storytelling, this program fails to show

LOOK HERE

To watch the "Crossroad" video by Makoto Shinkai, go to:

**www.youtube.com/
watch?v=M4QeeP8bI3c**

how it helps students get accepted into college and the main purpose may not be grasped by the audience.

Z-Kai is a cram school that provides correspondence courses to any student from preschoolers to college students, but this particular commercial focuses on third year high school students living in Japan getting ready to take entrance exams for college. When the commercial introduces Shouta's story, a girl in the background asks, "Isn't he a student testing for college? How does he study?" The commercial's arrangement grabs the attention of busy high school students. Between the 45 and 50 second marks, Shouta is shown working on worksheets that he received from Z-Kai at home. The company presents this to state that a student unable to go to a designated location is still able to obtain the help he or she wants. This also shows that Z-Kai understands students of different backgrounds and aims to help them. When an old man points out that the island that Miho lives on does not have a cram school that can help her with her studies, the commercial demonstrates how Z-Kai recognizes students in similar situations. Without Z-Kai, students like Miho and Shouta might struggle to find the help they desire in order to enter a college of their choice due to their personal backgrounds. This commercial focuses on top schools like Tokyo University. The company chooses Tokyo University to demonstrate that if a student joins Z-Kai, the chance of getting accepted into a good college increases.

Not only does the company recognize its audience, it also knows how to appeal to the viewers' emotions by using animation and storytelling. In Japan, many people of all ages watch anime, a popular type of media. Middle school students to young adults especially enjoy anime as it contains creative stories, relatable characters, and interesting themes, which add to anime's popularity. In addition, anime includes a variety of genres that can appeal to anyone in some way. Because of its popularity, more people are more likely to stay and

LOOK HERE

You can read more about Japanese cram schools on this blog post:

http://www.tofugu.com/2013/11/12/lets-talk-about-japanese-cram-school/

watch the Z-Kai commercial rather than flip to a different channel. If a person stays for the commercial, he or she can relate to the characters introduced in it. In "Z-Kai: Crossroad," the audience sees that Miho and Shouta are high school students who endure steps that real high school students in Japan have to experience before college. In the beginning of the commercial, Miho and Shouta do not possess special reasons to attend college and never promise anyone that they will go. The two express the need to enter college to search for a goal. High school students in real life can relate to this, as they start to set objectives for themselves and their futures. Miho and Shouta believe that they can find that goal in college despite their predicaments like not living nearby a cram school or having a part-time job. With the help of Z-Kai, determined Miho and Shouta take the Tokyo University entrance exam. While the two students await their results, the tutor that grades Shouta's and Miho's assignments at Z-Kai wonders whether or not Miho and Shouta got accepted to college. By showing the tutor's thoughts, it reveals that Z-Kai workers care for their students and want to help them succeed. Viewers that see this will find this interesting and consider Z-Kai as a place to go seek help and eventually achieve whatever goal they have in mind, just like Miho and Shouta did.

Although this commercial expresses an array of emotions, it fails to state its claim in a straightforward way. Since the commercial implies its message, the audience may miss the objective that Z-Kai tries to deliver. Anime usually has elements of story and deep characters that draw the attention of viewers; however, "Z-Kai: Crossroad" has an uneven balance between emotion and underlying meaning. The story of the commercial overshadows the purpose. At first, this commercial does not look like an advertisement; instead, it resembles a trailer for an upcoming anime film that someone should look forward to. When I first saw this commercial, I needed my friend to explain to me that it was a commercial for a cram school, not an anime trailer. The story and colors pulled me away from the main purpose. The commercial's approach distracts the audience and therefore viewers lose themselves in the story rather than what the commercial truly wants to convey.

In addition to the implicit message, the commercial fails to provide enough information about the company's product to fully convince customers to register for Z-Kai. It does not include specifics about the company's tutoring methods or success rates, for example. The commercial explains that Z-Kai sends supplemental work to the tutee's residence but neglects to mention the type of material or amount of work sent. This leaves viewers with questions like, "Is this program right for me," or, "Do they expect me to find out more on their website or something?" This beautiful commercial leaves these types of questions unanswered, adding to the confusing message. In addition, the logo of Z-Kai appears in a few parts of the video as well as at the end, but in small sized print. By making the logo small, viewers may look past the logo and forget about the company. The company assumes that potential customers will research more information, but this commercial implies that they do not need further research because the audience may be already lost in the storyline and ignoring the company as a whole. Z-Kai ineffectively informs its audience about itself in this commercial and makes the viewers wonder why a commercial like "Z-Kai: Crossroad" exists.

Analysis

In the commercial "Z-Kai: Crossroad," the audience goes on a journey for two minutes as they follow the story of high school students preparing for college entrance exams. This commercial utilizes and relies largely on detailed animation and a compelling story to grab viewers' attention and encourage them to enroll in Z-Kai. Although the components of the commercial may aid in persuading the audience, it does not give enough information about the company to back up why students should pick Z-Kai over other programs. This commercial left me wondering why I should bother signing up for something that depends greatly on appealing visuals rather than showing facts that back up the overall claim. I found the commercial very interesting and fun to watch, but it leaves me with questions yet to be answered.

Lydia Kwong is a Food Science major.

Works Cited

Z会 「クロスロード」 120 秒 Ver. *YouTube.* Youtube, 25 Feb. 2014. Web. 13 April 2014.

CONSIDER THIS

- When analyzing a text readers might not be familiar with, it's important to briefly summarize and describe the text. Can you locate a summary of the commercial in this essay? In other words, is the summary condensed into one section of the paper, or is it interspersed throughout the analysis? Does this rhetorical choice work?

- At one point, Kwong explains that anime is often implicit in its storytelling and seems to suggest that employing anime for commercial purposes may not be effective. Discuss this claim further with your classmates and consider whether or not anime is the most effective style for a commercial that is trying to persuade Japanese students to enroll in a tutoring program.

- This commercial was designed and directed by well-known anime artist Makoto Shinkai and was recently included in a museum exhibit devoted to the artist's work. The writer of this essay does not focus upon the fact that the commercial was created by a critically acclaimed anime artist. Does knowing that information alter the analysis of the commercial at all? If so, how or why?

"Doublethinking" Apple and the "1984" Ad

Cameron Montalvo

On January 24, 1984, Apple introduced the Macintosh, a revolutionary technology that forever changed our relationship with the digital world and the consumption of information. Days before the historic product's release, a dramatic and controversial 1984-themed Super Bowl XVIII commercial shocked millions of viewers across the world who were undoubtedly caught off-guard from the predictable ads for various beers, cars, and fast foods. This bizarre sixty-second clip subtly yet effectively introduced Apple's new personal computer through its unprecedentedly blunt and provocative style. Strongly based off of the famous 1949 George Orwell novel and subsequent motion picture, the Macintosh, with the great success of its Super Bowl commercial, undoubtedly changed that year and many years that followed. At the end of the ad, the clip even boldly pledged to its technologically primitive 1980's viewers, "You'll see why 1984 won't be like '*1984*'" (Apple). At the time, it would have been impossible to completely realize the implications of

> **LOOK HERE**
>
> Watch Apple's "1984" ad here:
>
> **https://www.youtube.com/watch?v=axSnW-ygU5g**

this radically confrontational ad and its product, but today it is clear to virtually everyone that Apple's products have immensely changed the world. Despite this, the audiences of this incredibly successful T.V. commercial, old and new, are still coming to terms with the subtle messages and themes embedded in the ad. Within a setting that parallels Orwell's *1984*, Apple's Macintosh advertisement thoroughly captured the attention of the Super Bowl's audience and countless others through its timelessly relevant appeal to totalitarian fears and the contrasting technological heroism that symbolized the Macintosh personal computer.

In this ominous context, Apple capitalized greatly through the commercial's effective fear-instilling strategy. From the opening scene, viewers were thrown right into an eerie and emotionally stirring setting. Dramatic camera angles of homogenized and expressionless henchmen introduced the convincing and persisting dystopian vibes. With their ghostly gray jumpsuits and pale faces, they marched in synchronicity down a narrow corridor lined with bright, loud, and engaging propagandist screens. From the very beginning of the ad, the soundscape was immediately inundated with factory horns, the thuds of marching feet, and a dictating voice in the middle of a televised speech. The speaker's military-esque face is masked with aviator glasses and can be seen on countless screens within the corridor and throughout the advertisement. The screens appeared as some sort of computer-television hybrid and were littered with obscure symbols and codes as they broadcasted the man's message. He cryptically praised some kind of vague techno-eugenic conformity via the ubiquitous Orwellian "tele-screens", saying, "Today marks the first anniversary of the glorious information purification directives" (Apple). This allusion to 1984's dictatorial "Big Brother" pervades the commercial and thoroughly evokes pathos with these types of countless fear-driving features.

This approach, albeit controversial, was actually a remarkably effective and legitimate strategy. Research has demonstrated that advertisers can significantly increase the interest and persuasiveness of commercials through the incorporation of fear tactics (Hyman and Tansey 108). Additionally, this research also points to empirical evidence that indicates better recollection of products from ads that portray fear. Because of this value in appeals to fear, Apple maintained those particular thematic efforts in its commercial through many other more subtle qualities. A multifaceted example of this intention to invoke fear in its audience can be seen in the perpetual strictly gray/blue color-scheme and dark industrial backdrop. These components provide an essential pseudo-futuristic foundation for the content. These dystopian stylistic decisions are also hallmarks of the commercial's director, Ridley Scott. His dystopian style of cinematography is clearly successful in his other works such as *Blade Runner* from 1982. Ultimately, in this case, these decisions contribute to an additional, subtler intention for the psychology and logic of the CBS audience. University of Illinois professor Linda M. Scott (unrelated to Ridley Scott) describes it as a form of reverse-psychology, where "the set is an important element in the logic of the commercial: symptomatic of the apparently illogical... pattern of the imagery and the argument" (75). The society is run-down and gloomy; yet the prevalent mentality being portrayed irrationally glorifies this dystopia and the abundant "technology" that has contributed to its "success." This weak logic steadily instills technophobia coupled with anxiety for the future of the commercial and real life. It is from this psychological framework that the Macintosh computer is eventually introduced and is successfully marketed in the commercial.

In the midst of this ironically shabby yet futuristic environment, a new, highly juxtaposed figure takes the stage. It is a young woman, played by the attractive athlete Anya Major, running in slow motion down another similar narrow corridor. Her distinctness is clear; her vibrant tan, healthy complexion, and muscular tone immediately shatter the color-scheme and the sense of dullness and lifelessness that envelop the set of the opening half of the commercial. Wearing a bright white tank top, neon orange runner's shorts, and holding a large sledgehammer, she is chased by armed officials as she runs toward a central auditorium-like room that closely resembles the opening scene of the *1984* motion picture. Her presence immediately becomes the target of the viewer's attention.

Not surprisingly, her presence is also a comprehensive symbol of the Macintosh, not just figuratively, but literally too. Her white top is embellished with a rudimentary corporate sketch of the Macintosh that glows from the main "telescreen" of the auditorium. She makes her way through the rows of conformed, mindless, and reactionless minions of the massive "Big Brother" figure on the screen before stopping abruptly. With only a few suspenseful seconds to spare, she spins the sledgehammer around her body several times before throwing it directly at the center of the auditorium's screen producing a massive flash of light that engulfs the now visibly captivated and responsive audience in the room.

Comparable to the heroine figure destroying the screen that dictated conformity, Apple and the Macintosh personal computer deconstructed consumers' perceptions of conformity, enabling them to dictate their own identity in an entirely unprecedented manner. In this regard, "the ad's rhetoric of freedom and revolution is used to constitute consumers" (Stein 1) and their new and desirable liberties brought about by the Macintosh. This symbolic action of destroying the telescreen also acted as a means for Apple, a relatively unknown computer manufacturer at the time, to establish an emotionally founded credibility as a company that consumers could support. Apple was in a position that lacked ethos, so the use of this incredibly influential commercial allowed the company to effectively reach out to a massive and impressionable audience. In this sense, as an incredibly small underdog in the market for computers, Apple's commercial also metaphorically dissented from the conformity of its industry, which was dominated by technologies developed by IBM. Moreover, Apple's Macintosh, along with countless of their future products, have come to thoroughly break down consumers' perception about technological and social paradigms.

When this radical advertisement concluded, the 1984 Super Bowl viewers were hurled right back out of the 1984 state of mind and were put back into "football" mode without a moment to pause and reflect. When that reflection eventually happened, there was a dramatic consensus: people were marveling more at the unprecedented marketing styles than at Apple's unprecedentedly user-friendly machines. Despite this, the Macintosh became a hugely successful product, and "The 1984 Commercial" has since been hailed as one of the best ads of all time. The tremendously strong emotional appeals that are tied to the horrors of Orwellian dystopia, in conjunction with Anya Major's heroic depiction of the Macintosh computer, ultimately made this incredibly persuasive rhetoric into the famous and memorable commercial that it quickly became.

Cameron Montalvo is a Soil Science major.

Analysis

Works Cited

1984. Dir. Micheal Radford. Umbrella-Rosenblum Films Production. Dec. 1984.

"1984 (advertisement)." *Wikipedia.* Wikimedia Foundation, 06 Nov. 2014. Web. 11 June 2014. Apple. CBS. 22 Jan. 1984. Television.

Hyman, Michael R., and Richard Tansey. "The Ethics of Psychoactive Ads." *Journal of Business Ethics* 9.2 (1990): 105–14. Web.

Orwell, George. *1984.* New York: Signet Classic, 1950.

"Ridley Scott." *Wikipedia.* Wikimedia Foundation, 06 Sept. 2014. Web. 11 June 2014.

Scott, Linda M. "'For the Rest of Us': A Reader-Oriented Interpretation of Apple's '1984' Commercial." *The Journal of Popular Culture* 25.1 (1991): 67–81. Web.

Stein, Sarah R. "The '1984' Macintosh Ad: Cinematic Icons and Constitutive Rhetoric in the Launch of a New Machine." *Quarterly Journal of Speech* 88.2 (2002): 169–92. Web.

CONSIDER THIS

- For this analysis, Montalvo has to connect numerous texts and time periods: the 1984 Superbowl, Orwell's *1984*, the movie *1984*, and of course the Apple commercial. Does he successfully synthesize these different components?

- This analysis focuses on the advertisement's ethos and pathos. How might an analysis of logos complicate or enhance the essay?

Who or what has been—or could be—influential in your life?

You can learn a lot by asking people questions and by looking at locations with fresh eyes, but you may need to slow down and observe your surroundings through a new lens. The authors featured in this section have done exactly that.

CONSIDER THIS

- The following four images were taken around San Luis Obispo. Each image offers a different angle—or lens—through which to view the area's culture, history, and stories. Study the images and their captions to get differing glimpses into this region. Moreover, as you write your own profile essay, think carefully about the angle that you select.

- If you were to create a "photo essay" profiling San Luis Obispo—or even Cal Poly—what kinds of images would you select?

This "Iron Road Pioneers" sculpture, created by Elizabeth MacQueen, "honors the enormous contribution of the Chinese immigrants who helped build the early railroads on the Central Coast and across the nation" (monument plaque). The monument stands in front of the SLO railway station.

Photograph by Brenda Helmbrecht

Another beautiful day at the Pacific Ocean, near Morro Bay.

Photograph by Annie Garner

This fountain stands in front of the San Luis Obispo de Tolosa Mission. In the 1700s, when the mission was built, bears dominated the region. According to its plaque, the "fountain gives voice to the Chumash and wildlife that instilled this valley with the rhythms of spirit and love."

Photograph by Brenda Helmbrecht

"Bubblegum Alley" in downtown San Luis Obispo, is a popular tourist destination, one that has been profiled in news outlets across the country. Some visitors find the alley repulsive, while others find it quirky and fun.

Photograph by Brenda Helmbrecht

Almost Heaven

Nicholai Busch

Reflective Memo: *When I first embarked on writing this essay, I was initially troubled with what to write about. Talking to my friend, Kelly, soon changed that. After the full interview I knew I really wanted to capture the story that she just told me about a hitchhiking trip she was on. My first draft was just that, I focused more on the story than I did Kelly. After our peer reviews, and through the course of my editing, I changed the focus of the essay. Instead of focusing on the actual trip as the subject, I used the trip as an example of the subject, Kelly. When writing about hitchhiking it may be difficult to convince your audience that it can be a cool thing to do. In my initial draft, my main support consisted of all the physical elements of the trip. After my revising I focused on the mental parts of the trip. I dove into Kelly's feelings about art and strangers and used that as my subject for the essay. As I told the narrative of the trip in the background of the essay, I used the foreground to talk about the emotions behind each part of the trip and how they explain why Kelly enjoys hitchhiking so much. Since the profile essay needed to profile Kelly better, I think it really helped to dive into the secrets of the mind.*

After adding a lot more about the feelings behind hitchhiking, I actually took out some details from the trip only to push it back as just an example for explaining why Kelly does this. Since I already had a very detailed example, I now have detailed support for my main subject. I was able to change the perspective essentially.

I also noticed that I tend to write sentences with a lot of extra words in them. This I attempted to clean up a bit my second time around. Along with extra words, I used the word "you" quite a bit in my first draft, which is something I also worked to clean up. With a few of these grammatical weaknesses I definitely make up for it with the essays' content. Hitchhiking and adventure are always exciting because there are so many possibilities, there's really no "cookie-cutter" outline for an adventure story. Overall, I am very happy with how this profile essay turned out.

"I sprinted up to the car with one hand on some pepper spray and the other poised on the pocketknife concealed in my jeans. I guess there is still a part of me that feels the need to be cautious when approaching a car with strangers in it. I never have been able to just let go completely and trust that the driver has good intentions, but I know I could defend myself if I had to." Those were Kelly's words as she described climbing in the rumbling Ford pickup that pulled over to the side of the road. She was feeling both anxious and excited to start a new hitch-hiking adventure. It's easy to hop in a car and drive somewhere for the weekend, but when hitching a ride with someone else to go to a destination that has yet to be determined, it takes on a whole new challenge.

I have known Kelly for many years and we've been on countless outdoor adventures throughout high school together. Starting with just day hikes and ending with weekend long spontaneous excursions to unknown places, I've learned that Kelly knows what she is doing.

Not very many people dedicate themselves to adventure the way she does. When I asked her to tell me about her most rewarding hitchhiking trip, she didn't hesitate to think of one. Many people are wary of hitchhiking because of how risky it can be; an unknown driver picking up unknown passengers opens up a lot of room for calamities. Usually, drivers and passengers have the best intentions, yet one can never be too careful. For a hitchhiker, taking a step out into the unknown can either make or break a trip; in Kelly's case, it turned a weekend excursion into an eye-opening adventure that gave her the very reason she does it.

The trip began early on April 18th of 2013, when Kelly decided that a journey south was needed to escape the busy college atmosphere. Kelly had been hitchhiking a few times before, but that didn't make her an expert at it. There

LOOK HERE

The Greater Good: A Hitchhiking Documentary offers a glimpse at the journey of one hitchhiker who thumbs his way through 13 countries:

http://documentaryaddict.com/The+Greater+Good +A+Hitchhike+Perspective-11728-doc.html

was always going to be a certain level of risk involved, which is part of the reason she does it. Hitchhiking eliminates every residual quantity of control that someone could have while traveling. To some, this might sound outright stupid, but to Kelly, it's an invitation for adventure. Bringing her friend Zach along on the weekend trip, the two fastened on their 50 Liter backpacks full of gear and started walking up Exit 14's onramp along I-5 North, just outside of Ashland, Oregon. Almost immediately after displaying the universal sign of a thumbs up, pointed in the direction of travel, the large Ford pickup pulled over. Their first goal of the trip was to get to Grants Pass, about 45 minutes north of Ashland. Despite the relatively short distance, it took 3 separate car rides to reach their destination.

Part of the reason that Kelly started hitchhiking is that there is almost no planning necessary. It's one of the few activities where almost no input can yield an extraordinary output. There are no hotel reservations, flights to book, or schedules to be confined to. Wherever the driver drops her off is where she has to make camp. Sometimes she'll get lucky and hitch a ride half-way across the state; whereas, other times she won't make it ten minutes before having to signal for another driver. From Grants Pass the two caught a ride along the 199 to Cave Junction with a 24-year-old woman they nicknamed Honey-Mexico. Kelly explained, "When I hitchhike for a long distance and have lots of drivers, it is often easier for me to remember someone by what they talked about rather than remembering a generic name. This driver talked about beehives and her plans to go to Mexico." The characters she has met have always proved to be interesting in some way.

Except for the occasional super-quiet driver, there is always something fascinating to talk about. Once again left on the street they approached their next ride that had pulled over, a blue van. They could see that a middle-aged woman was driving and what looked like her father riding shotgun. When they opened the door to get in, four giant dogs greeted them with slobbery faces and extended tongues. Also crammed in the back was an electric wheel chair left to roll around, which turned out to be for the father, who was paralyzed. Kelly has always been an animal lover, and, most of all, a dog lover. Whenever there are animals in the car, that picks her up; she knows that it will be a good ride. So when she saw the four dogs, it couldn't have been better. Hopping in next to the dogs, Kelly and Zach rode along until reaching Crescent City. The woman and her father dropped them off 50 yards away from the crashing waves of the Pacific Ocean.

With the sun setting over the water and the temperature beginning to drop, the two decided to scout around for a place to sleep. When Kelly goes on an adventure, she doesn't waste time with hotels or houses to spend the night in. Finding a secluded, covered spot in the forest or under a bridge is just as good. She finds comfort in places that offer the bare essentials of a shelter. It's like going back in time to where that's all that mattered, a roof overhead and walls to block the wind or fend off attackers. This primal instinct to find refuge is exemplified while hitchhiking. In a sense it's not about traveling anymore, it's about survival. As the trip evolves into a test of her abilities, Kelly puts recreational thoughts aside and narrows her search for a place to sleep. This time, their camp resided under some bleachers on a fair ground. Some cover above them and enough foliage around offered protection. After purchasing some nachos for dinner and peppermint lattes for dessert, they called it a night after their long day of travel.

Kelly woke early the next morning just as the sun began to peak up over the horizon. Starting the day at the same time the sun does only reinforces the feeling of survival. "There are some things you can't get away with while hitchhiking and one of them is sleeping in. When the earth awakens at dawn, so do you" said Kelly. Spending most of the day in Crescent City, Kelly and Zach started walking north along Highway 101 around 2 pm. Three miles up the road they stopped and stuck out their thumbs to signal for a ride.

Two hours later, in the heat of the day, the two began to question the possibility of making it anywhere. As if hitchhiking isn't risky enough, it can be just as bad if nobody even offers a ride. The two had planned on making their way back to Ashland that day, but it was already approaching late afternoon and they knew they didn't want to be caught on the side of the highway after dark. Another 30 minutes later, a small white bus emerged from the heat waves of the black pavement in the distance. Just like from a scene in a movie, the little bus grew larger as it drew nearer. It slowed and stopped just up the road from where Kelly was signaling. As they approached the vehicle they could see that there was a huge flag with a peace sign on it hanging out the window. The doors opened and the beat of reggae music spilled out into the street. Inside were eight other passengers and five large dogs this time! The two climbed up and found a seat, "as we got moving, Zach and I couldn't stop smiling! We hit the jackpot! Our ride was amazing and taking us all the way back over the Oregon border." The sheer excitement she was feeling when they drove off in the bus was unparalleled, the same feeling a young child might have when opening a birthday present; Kelly felt it every time she met someone new on a trip. Instead of a new toy, she was rewarded with inspiring personalities and pure delight. They were soon told that the group of travelers was from a hippie commune they called Almost Heaven. As the day grew closer to an end, the group invited the newly welcomed travelers to stay at their property that night. With such an enticing offer they couldn't refuse, Kelly graciously accepted.

Pulling into Almost Heaven a short while after, Kelly couldn't believe what she was seeing. She was standing in a sanctuary of wanderlust explorers that had come together to live as one. With cats and dogs running freely around the property, Kelly took a moment to process what was in front of her. There was a massive rainbow colored house with a proportionally sized fire pit out front. Being an artist herself, she was immediately fascinated by the vibrant walls of the house. It looked as if someone loaded paint buckets into a cannon and blasted the siding with random colors. If Kelly wasn't off exploring then she was drawing or painting. Art had been her way of communicating ever since she was a young girl. She had an eye for seeing something from a perspective that no one else could see. Hitchhiking trips give her a perspective on life that most don't even know exist. Stripping away the confines of society and breaking everything down into the bare essentials is what fuels her ambition for these trips. When she laid eyes on Almost Heaven, it defined every reason she had for hitchhiking. Everyone lived together in the house and ate together around the fire they were told. Kelly was warmly invited to join them for dinner, "It was one of the coolest, most unexpected, experiences I've ever had," she said. Unexpected being the operative word there, because if it were expected then it wouldn't be nearly as appreciated. Their second night was spent sharing stories and spreading smiles next to the bonfire.

"It was amazing to witness such kind-hearted people completely opening up their house to total strangers." I remember the first time Kelly told me this story, how perfect it all sounded. If only more people could see and appreciate the simplistic generosity that others have. Once again they packed their bags and slung them over their shoulders. Loading up in a Jeep, they were driven back into Grants Pass before waving goodbye to their newly made friends. From there, a Nigerian man drove them all the way onto campus, dropping them off in front of the dorms. With such a modest ending to a deep and meaningful trip, Kelly spent the rest of the day contemplating the events that had transpired. They expressed a way of life that she had been attracted to but didn't know how to describe. Each story she has gives another reason why she does it all in the first place. "The trip was everything I could have asked for and so much more! The unpredictability of the journey and the kindness of strangers is what keeps me hitting the road to this day." She realized that an adventure like the one she just partook in could only happen when traveling into the unknown and uncertain, making it possible to reach a place called Almost Heaven.

Nicholai Busch is an Industrial Technology major.

Work Cited

Sosa, Kelly. Personal Interview. 2 October 2013.

CONSIDER THIS

- In his "Reflective Memo," Busch discusses his revision process at length. How does his process compare to your own? What steps do you take when you revise?

- Busch begins his essay by alluding to his subject's fears. How does this focus influence the overall tone of the essay? Does it create an effective contrast with the joy Kelly feels at the end of the essay?

You Are Not a Still Image

Jennifer Berg

Reflective Memo: *I struggled through this paper, and struggled with the message of this paper in my life—as I hope any reader of it will. I know I could never fully do Spencer justice with just this gathering of words, because there are so many stories he has to tell, but hopefully I portrayed him clearly enough. Spencer is my boyfriend and I chose to leave our relationship out because I really wanted the paper to focus on his story and his personal journey, which came long before me. His words are very challenging and honest—ringing true to most of us who are trying to figure out what we are going to pursue for the next handful of years leading into the rest of our lives. They are words that are important for everyone to hear and at least consider no matter what stage of life they are settled in. It has truly been a privilege to share one of the many unique stories of an individual other than myself, and a great reminder that every human being has a story as complex and mysterious as my own.*

He struggles with words. Ask him a question and he gets quiet, weighing each individual word. Rewind a few years and Spencer Hobbs is sitting in a classroom with a tutor, teaching him the correct pronunciations: how to say R's and S's and so on. It's frustrating, but he fights through it, and speaks the words until they feel and sound right rolling off his tongue.

"I hate English," I heard him say recently, but when I ask him about his childhood and his first moments with creating, he launches with that deep voiced, laughter filled tone into memories of drawing picture stories. He'd grab printer paper and draw countless illustrations with short sentences dashing across the pages here and there. He'd staple them all together, and add it the growing pile—filling up boxes and boxes of these stapled stacks of stories. He shows me the way he painted flowers in only second grade and they are more beautiful than anything I could paint even now: the purples of the petals, the curve of each flower—advanced, but with the subtle edge of childhood that only childhood could create. I smile at the unavoidable story it tells and agree, "English can be difficult."

His speech impediment is long gone now, only cropping up in certain phrases, but his thoughts still dwell on the words, weighing them, until they feel and sound right on his tongue. He speaks carefully, and maybe that's what I see now—an eloquent speaker—not because speech comes easily, but because it does not. So I ask him if he felt more comfortable communicating through art.

He starts in, "I definitely felt more confident in it. Even when it came to school—whenever we did arts and crafts I actually felt like a good student in those times, rather than when we'd do English or History, I would feel stupid.

I didn't see art as a way to communicate until middle school when we could choose a whole class dedicated to doing art. So once I got there, I saw expressionism. I fell in love with expressionist art . . . which to me means you're portraying an emotion or concept with your art. It's not just a still image."

Rewind a few years and his father is pressing his forehead up against Spencer's, screaming his usual insults: "YOU'RE A DEMON CHILD. YOU RUIN EVERYTHING." He feels the hardness of his father's skull, the old familiar words scraping into his, sinking, etching deep into the fabric of his soul. Later he'll sit down to paint and what comes out is trees bent around in unnatural curves surrounding a secluded bench in a quiet field. Surreal, because the curvature of the trees cannot happen in nature, but expressionist because he's longed for a quiet world to his own. Just a quiet place to rest for a while, an escape, a place where the loudness of the words cannot reach him. It's not just a still image.

High School is over now, and pursuing anything to do with art makes Spencer's Father scoff, "There's no money in that." So without obvious support from his parents, Spencer went searching for a job that did have money in it. Thus the year of the EMT.

"Working as an EMT felt like taking the color out of life," he says darkly, and now we rewind to his typical day. He wakes up—wakes up early to mentally prepare himself, making sure he's thirty minutes early to sit in the car and pray that he has a good day. *Start a shift, a 72-hour shift. Rig check. Have all the equipment you need. You have scheduled calls. You are sitting around waiting for the next call, stressed out of your mind. Get that call, get in the zone. You take care of patients very well, very fast, and very effectively. As soon as you are out of the situation, go right back to stressing. Even at night when you are allowed sleep, you sleep maybe two-three hours. All the while you are anxious about the phone going off. Outside of work—isolation. You see so much pain in the world, moment to moment, pain and horror, and you are weary of others and their petty problems. Suddenly it's hard to care. Hard to care about much else of anything.*

"I want to make everything visually beautiful and I couldn't even write the way I wanted to," he recalls. He was numb. Work took up the majority of time and art was out of the question. The weekend would hit and he would de-stress by sitting and watching football mindlessly, a sport he has always hated. Numb, so very numb. So his mentors saw him suffering and encouraged him to leave the job, as it was destructive to him. Two job opportunities cropped up, and thus the BIO Tech job.

In the BIOtech job, you are using your eyes nine hours for the day—your job is your eyes. You're just looking at this ugly shit all day. No windows. It's pitch black in the room. All that lights the room is the inspection booths. The only good design in these inspection booths is that it is black and white. Sit. Receive sample, shake and look for unwanted particles. Shake. Sit. Stare. Shake. Sit. Stare. Move on. Work 12 hours today to get that overtime. More money. Too tired for friends. Hour drive, gym, cook, sleep.

"Now," he laughs, "I don't have a typical day anymore—and that's what I love. Now I have enough free time to create and spend time at Riptide," a Church Middle school group of which he is a leader. I see him interact with the middle-schoolers—see him care about their lives and tear up when they stand and talk to the crowd of other students about overcoming their struggles. When he speaks, his voice is clear and wise, and I see that they admire and look up to him. They are able to joke with him and they are able to lean on him for support.

You see, tired of investing his life into a numbing money machine, he quit his BIOtech job, took a leap of faith, and finally decided to go back to school for Graphic Design. His job interning with the Youth Pastor, Jared, is to create titles and images that connect to the series at Church (a theme as they go through certain stories in the Bible). Soon, with the extra time in his life, he volunteered to lead a small group and Jared soon saw Spencer's natural ability to lead. Despite his struggle with words,

LOOK HERE

Take time out to explore your own creativity at the ASI Craft Center on campus.

http://www.asi.calpoly.edu/craft_center

and despite his fear of not being able to love the kids well because of the way his father treated him growing up, he speaks, he leads, and he creates. It's been a very long process and he still struggles saying, "I've never been the best painter, or the best sculptor or anything. I compared myself to others and they have so much natural talent. How would I ever be able to compete with them?" His initial launch into graphic design, while he likes working with hands more than anything, was a way to not have to be the best drawer or painter or best sculptor, but he could use technology to create art. "I thought that it would solve my insecurity of not being the best artist, but as I became more serious and actually really passionate about Graphic Design, it was hard not to compare myself to others who had so much more natural talent in this field." Maybe that's what I see now, watching his face break into a smile every other sentence, that he is so incredible not because everything came easily, but because it did not. It took time and growth—faith and risk.

"To me living your dream is doing what makes you come alive. I think that's what a dream is—it's like if you think 'what is your dream?' Well what do you *love* to do? It's the thing that makes you come alive. It makes you feel happy, makes you feel joy, and it is so life giving—so you're *full* and *alive*.... Does that phrase make sense? People have this big dream of being a famous musician or artist or actor or poet, and I think people with dreams that have to do with creativity especially—they start to think they can't do it. So they go to college, and get a career, and work, and then they stop doing the thing that makes them come alive because they don't think they'll ever reach that ultimate goal. I don't believe in that. I believe to be content in your life, whether that dream will come true or not, you have to make time to live into that dream. Does that answer the question? I don't even know." He laughs his usual laugh, and messes with his hair. The words may not come immediately, but he has thought about every one. And they are such beautiful words. So I smile, "Yes, it answers it perfectly."

Jennifer Berg is a Liberal Studies major.

CONSIDER THIS

- Berg employs a variety of stylistic choices—including italics, sentence fragments, and capital letters—to build a unique voice. How do these rhetorical choices affect your engagement with the essay? Are there any stylistic methods that you might consider using in your own essays?

- In her "Reflective Memo," Berg explains her reasons for keeping her relationship with Spencer out of the essay. How might your perception of Spencer change had she decided to frame him as her boyfriend?

Labor of Love

Kenna Sandberg

My eyes are drawn to the old wooden bucket with the stainless steel canister inside, surrounded by chunks of ice and clumps of rock salt. I cannot wait any longer. The urge to dig in and take the first spoonful is upon me. I watch as my dad begins to take the lid off the canister and slowly pull the dasher out. My mouth begins to water as I frantically search for a spoon. Without hesitation, I dig right in and take the first bite. Its cold sensation sends a chill through my body, and I cannot resist a second spoonful. By now, everyone has pushed their way through to the dasher to get a taste of the freshly churned ice cream.

Since the 1930s, the White Mountain Ice Cream Maker has been a part of the Sandberg family, creating memories and bringing us closer together. My great grandparents, Elizabeth and Edward Sandberg were the start of it all. Each Sunday during the summer months they would make ice cream, enjoying each other's company and laughter. Once the ice cream had been made and everyone went about their business for the day, my grandpa Norman would sit outside with the family dog and work his way through the ice cream, practically eating the whole thing. When my dad was young, he would sit on the ice cream maker while his dad cranked away. He sat, waiting impatiently, ready to enjoy the cool feeling the ice cream gave him. Hearing my dad share his memories of the ice cream maker makes me think of mine. One of my fondest memories of making ice cream is arguing with my brother to see who could last the longest at the crank arm. Most of the time I would push through to the end, but occasionally he would last just a bit longer than I did. These are just a few of the many memories that I cherish and will one day share with my children as we make ice cream together as a family.

Making ice cream has always been a tradition in the Sandberg Family. As my dad says, "We can be found making ice cream at the drop of a hat." Our family has not only made ice cream for the enjoyment, but also for special occasions,

LOOK HERE

Get a glimpse of the ice cream maker the Sandberg family uses to build memories at **http://www.whitemountainproducts.com**

including my grandma and grandpa's wedding anniversary, my high school graduation party, and family gatherings. With a glimmer in his eye, my dad states that "the ice cream maker represents the importance of family, bringing us closer together each time we use it. It also symbolizes a labor of love."

The process of making ice cream is not quick and easy; it takes time and preparation as each of us takes part in producing the final product. Before anything can happen, the wooden bucket must be soaked in water in order for the wood to expand. Once the wood has soaked for a day or so, my mom and I follow the family recipe, mixing all the ingredients together and pouring them into the canister. My dad and brother gather the ice and rock salt that surrounds the canister; they create the brine that solidifies the liquid cream into ice cream. As my dad sits in anticipation, cranking the ice cream maker, all he can think about "is eating off the dashing and enjoying the wonderful homemade ice cream." When it starts to get harder and harder to crank, that means the ice cream is close to done. The whole process to creating this masterpiece takes around an hour to an hour and a half. It requires time and dedication, but in the end it is worth it.

It's finally time to eat off the dasher. This is the moment we have all been waiting for. As my dad slowly pulls the dasher from the canister, he states with excitement in his voice, "Grab your spoons and get ready to dig in." The second he places the dasher down, I can hear the clinking of spoons as we fight to get ourselves some of the delicious ice cream. Once the dasher has been "licked clean" as my dad would say, it is time to dish ourselves a bowl, and add some toppings; the most popular one is sugared pecans. As we sit enjoying our bowl of ice cream, it occurs to me that such a small item can bring our family so close. I love being able to see my family enjoying our time together all because of a White Mountain Ice Cream Maker that has been passed down from generation to generation.

With love and tenderness in his voice, my dad expresses that "seeing a family tradition being passed down to the next generation brings great joy and excitement to [his] heart. Knowing that [he] will be able to share this with [his] grandchildren is amazing; they will become a part of this tradition and will pass it on to their kids." The White Mountain Ice Cream Maker symbolizes a labor of love and compassion for one another, bringing we Sandbergs closer through the generations. Most people would run to the store to have ice cream, but the Sandberg family loves making it. It is a process that all of us are able to participate in, creating memories and sharing laughs. It is not about the time and effort it requires, but the enjoyment of being with one another.

Kenna Sandberg is an Agricultural Communications major.

Work Cited

Sandberg, Kenton. Personal interview. 02 February 2014.

CONSIDER THIS

- In this essay, Sandberg uses an inanimate object to shed light on a larger subject: her family. How does her description of the ice cream maker allow her to organize her essay and expand on her relationship with her family?

- Repetition can enhance an essay's meaning. For instance, in this essay, the author relies heavily on the recurrence of "ice cream." Is this use of repetition effective? How could repetition be used differently?

How Pieces of Wood Can Touch Souls

Amanda Post

Reflective Memo: *It was really fun to write this essay. Katie McRaven, the subject of the profile, is my best friend back home, so it was cool to see her (via Skype) and catch up as well as find out more about the impact of playing violin on her life. I interviewed Katie, then immediately wrote the essay so it was fresh in my mind. It was also easier for me to write this essay because I also play violin and understand what she was talking about. I went through a similar experience: we both started playing violin at the same age. I like that my essay had a good flow overall and was cohesive. Connecting all the ideas I have in my head is sometimes a challenge for me.*

One evening, hundreds of people sit in rows of seats in a concert hall. They flip through their programs and converse quietly, generating a soft hum that fills the amphitheater. On stage, a "shell" made of wooden framework designed to enhance and project sound is set up, along with many chairs, arranged in rows to form a U-shape. The house lights slowly dim, and the chatter dies away. The audience sits in silence as the lights directed at the stage get brighter. Musicians dressed in tuxedos and floor-length dresses file on stage and set up their instruments. Once they are all seated, a man wearing a tailcoat emerges, signaling a rumble of applause from the audience. He takes a bow, then steps onto a podium and reveals his baton. He raises his arms, breathes in and gives a downbeat to the orchestra, starting the piece.

Katie McRaven has been performing on-stage in shows like this for eleven years. As a classical violinist, she thrives off the energy that comes from playing music on stage for hundreds of people. Katie began playing the violin in third grade, and is currently a member of the Cal State Long Beach Symphony Orchestra. She is a freshman in college, and attends CSULB as a biomedical engineering major. When she first picked up the violin, she had no idea that she would end up pursuing it as far as she has. "In the third grade," Katie said, "we had the option to play violin or cello, and a ton of my friends were going to pick one to try out, so I decided to as well. I didn't know anything about either instrument, but I was remarkably sure that violin was what I wanted to play."

For the first half a year of learning, the new musicians were given a tissue box covered in wood-patterned wrapping paper with a painter's mixing stick attached to it as a violin, and a wooden stick as a bow. This was

LOOK HERE

For information about Cal Poly's Symphony, along with links to repertoire pieces, visit:
http://symphony.calpoly.edu

so that the kids could grasp the technique of holding a violin properly first, before actually starting to rent and use a real one. Even at age eight, Katie and her friends thought that sawing a piece of wood on a tissue box as practice was silly, but it piqued a curiosity in her that inspired her to stick with it to uncover more. Her defining moment was when she attended a concert starring Midori, a famous violinist, with her father. It was a mesmerizing experience, and he told her that one day, if she worked hard enough, that could be her. "Next thing I knew," Katie commented, "I was in eighth grade, going on to high school with no intention of ending my career as a violinist."

When it comes to how she got where she is today, Katie said that her story was different than most. "Anyone who's good at violin has been taking private lessons their whole life, but I didn't," she said with a smirk. Private lessons are violin lessons given to a student by a professional, usually once a week, to help them improve technique and sound. Good private lessons are often very expensive, which separates out a lot of the less-serious musicians. Growing up, Katie was always very conscientious about her parents spending money on her and insisted that they didn't need to provide private lessons for her. She instead went through ten years of orchestra on natural talent and practicing alone. As a freshman, she started out in the lowest tier of orchestras, for freshmen and beginners. She practiced for hours at home and made an effort during rehearsal; by the end of her junior year, her director finally asked her if she wanted to join the chamber orchestra. One of her greatest feats was making it into both the Long Beach Poly Chamber Orchestra and Long Beach All-District Orchestra her senior year of high school, which are known as two of the best orchestras in the Long Beach and Los Angeles area.

After Katie's interview, I was rewarded with the opportunity to see her play her violin. She owns a beautiful hand-crafted violin with tiger-striped wood, and a carbon fiber bow. When she took them out of her case, her eyes glittered with admiration, and it was obvious how much she loves what she does. She performed a transcribed version of the first Bach cello suite, a popular piece often used in commercials and movies. Katie was very humble about her talent, and had noticeably flushed cheeks upon finishing. Although she enjoys playing solo music, Katie said that she prefers to play in an ensemble.

Besides the obvious difficulty of learning how to individually work an instrument, being part of more advanced orchestras brings many new challenges to the table for musicians. The music is much more intricate, which increases the amount of time needed for members to learn the parts at home. "When you move on to more sophisticated playing, you need to be able to listen to those around you, and adjust accordingly on several different factors like volume, pitch, and phrasing," Katie said. She currently spends over four hours a week in rehearsal with her classmates, working on an hour's worth of music total. For their performance to sound professional, the orchestra needs to spend lots of time together, tuning chords individually and running through transitions to make them seamless. After mastering a piece, one of the most rewarding experiences is performing it for others, but being a part of an orchestra also offers opportunities to make new social connections and friends.

However, that's not all that comes from her violin career. When asked what else she values about playing the violin, Katie said that, "Classical music is more than just a hobby for me, it's become a huge part of my life; it keeps me sane… No matter what mood I'm in, a good classical song will immediately calm me down and put my mind at ease." Katie paused, looked down and smiled. Chuckling to herself with an air of wonder, she continued:

> I remember one time I was driving back from school after a really rough day, and I was playing 97.1, the classical music station in Long Beach. A few minutes before I pulled into my driveway, a really beautiful violin concerto by Vivaldi came on, and I was entranced by it. It was a twenty minute piece, but after parking my car, I just sat there without moving, listening to the whole thing through. Pieces like that go straight through my ears and touch my soul; it's one of the most beautiful and addicting feelings I know. When I hear certain melodies or chord progressions and resolutions, I feel tingly waves of pleasure shoot down my limbs to my fingertips and toes. Nothing else in life but music is capable of making me feel like that, which I am very grateful for.

Katie recommends that anyone who is interested in playing an instrument should go for it. She said that whenever she tells people that she plays violin many say that they "wish they were talented enough to play an instrument." But Katie argues that if she got to where she is by starting on a tissue box and stick, anyone willing to commit can learn to play an instrument, as well as reap the many benefits that come with it.

LOOK HERE

Even if you don't play the violin, you may still appreciate what goes into making and repairing them:

http://www.youtube.com/watch?v=8S_6twdF6-0

Amanda Post is a Biological Sciences major.

Work Cited

McRaven, Katie. Personal interview. 25 Jan. 2014.

CONSIDER THIS

- A block quotation—per MLA format, any quotation longer than four lines—is featured prominently near the end of this essay. What do you think of its inclusion here, and how do you think it relates to the surrounding text? As a writer, what factors should you take into account as you consider incorporating a longer quotation into an essay?

- In her Reflective Memo, Post explains that, "Connecting all the ideas I have in my head is sometimes a challenge…" What strategies does she use to achieve what she calls the "good flow" of the essay? Can you define "flow," and how important is "flow" to your perception of writing in general?

A Romance With Romance

Jillian Keegan

When I first heard that our long-standing family friend Mary McNear had written a book, I assumed it would be a comedy, memoir, or some combination of the two. She was always telling hilarious and colorful stories that left my whole family in stitches—like that time she spent $250 on medicine for the family hamster to improve his "quality of life," or once when she walked in on her sister and her sister's then-boyfriend, future president "Barry" Obama. If the book wasn't a comedic memoir, my next guess would have been literary fiction—Mary's mother was a published fiction author herself, and Mary had majored in English and history in college. I was therefore quite surprised to hear that the book she had penned was, in fact, a romance novel.

Romance—the literary genre that is perhaps viewed with more skepticism and criticism than any other—is actually the most popular genre in North America. A romance novel must satisfy two requirements: a love story must be the main focus of the plot, and the ending must be positive and satisfying. Though the basic structure of the romance novel is somewhat standardized, the form it takes can vary wildly. It can take place in any era; be set in any location, real or fictional, even science-fictional; and can fall anywhere from sweet and innocent to shockingly steamy. In 2012, romance fiction was an impressive $1.438 billion industry ("Romance Industry").

> ## LOOK HERE
>
> Go behind-the-scenes for a surprisingly thoughtful look at the artistry and consideration that goes into capturing an image for the cover of a romance novel: **http://www.youtube.com/watch?v=4x9G1osFrY8**

Despite the size of the industry, growing up in Mary's family, being a romance writer "was not considered an acceptable occupation… My parents, my mother, I should say, wanted me to be a college professor." Her family—especially her literary author mother—instilled in her the values of intellectual pursuits and hard work, so after majoring in English and history in college, she continued on the path that was expected of her and started a PhD in history.

However, Mary had actually known since adolescence that she wanted to write romance novels. "It was hard," she told me. "I kind of had to give up that dream, without ever admitting that that was my dream." When she talks about her time in college and grad school, it's clear she knew on some level that she was headed down the wrong path. "My heart wasn't really in it," she confessed. "It wasn't really what I wanted to be doing, but it was what I *was* doing, you know?"

Yet one can't help but wonder how far down that path she would have wandered had she not been interrupted by an unexpected obstacle. Her son, Harry, was born in 1995, the same year as me, and was in fact in my elementary school class. However, "when Harry was three," she explained, "I was writing my dissertation, and he was diagnosed with autism." Such a curveball lead her to reconsider her plans for not just her family, but herself. "I thought okay, this is going to be really challenging. This is not what I was expecting when I had a child, it's going to be much harder and there aren't going to be any guarantees and I don't know how this is going turn out, but I thought *you know what? I am going to do what I want to do for an hour a day.*" And what she wanted to do, what she had always really wanted to do, was write romance.

Of course, in practice this wasn't so simple. First, she had her personal struggles with the decision. She was still affected by her Midwestern Protestant upbringing, and by her memories of her mother's tortured process of writing literary fiction. She couldn't help feeling that, "if it was fun, either I couldn't be good at it, or I shouldn't be doing it." It was a challenge for her to overcome her deeply embedded aversion towards "doing something that wasn't intellectual, doing something that I thought was fun, doing something that I could enjoy and… you know, maybe even make money doing it."

Then, there was the matter of her inexperience. "This is like typically arrogant," she joked, confessing, "I started writing romance novels and I had never actually read one… I sort of had this preconceived notion of what they were like, and I wanted to do it my way." So perhaps it shouldn't be surprising that when she showed one of her early manuscripts to a literary agent, she received a response along the lines of, "It's obvious you've never read a romance novel before."

She didn't let this deter her. "I decided I was going to read— this was crazy—I was going read like one hundred romance novels. That was my plan. So I started reading them, and they were really bad!" She was an aspiring romance novelist, but even she was skepti-

LOOK HERE

Why are we so skeptical about romance novels? For an explanation of the genre's history, watch this brief multimedia composition, provocatively titled, "Dangerous Books For Girls: The Bad Reputation Of Romance Novels Explained":
http://www.youtube.com/watch?v=vKbYQhWhay0

cal of the romance novel. So she took the analytical skills she had learned as an undergraduate, and put them to use trying to figure out *why* those romance novels were so bad. She decided, "The biggest problem, from my perspective, was that they were boring… And I realized that every time a romance novel was boring, it was because one of two things was not happening in a scene. Either the scene wasn't revealing anything about a character, or the scene was not advancing the plot enough." So she set out to write a romance novel that did not fall prey to these two fatal errors.

She continued writing and honing her craft as Harry and her second child—Rose, a girl born three years later—grew up. Her goal was to "write romance novels for people who don't read romance novels," but that's not to say she departed from the features that make a novel a classic romance. "I knew I wasn't going to try to make them realistic," she told me, "the people are just exceptionally attractive, nobody worries about money…they live in this perfect small town." And though this idealism may be what causes some to scoff at the genre, Mary sees the value in such escapism. She told me a story about Rose and her friends getting ready for a high school dance last year, and how "they were trying on dresses and shoes and putting on makeup…and later I found out they all just danced with each other the whole night, so nothing happened, but I realized there was just like this excitement in the air, and I realized that in life, it's not about what really happens, it's about what might happen." That is the same energy she tries to capture in her books.

In December of 2012 Mary got her first three-book contract from HarperCollins for her "Butternut Lake" series, and the following spring her son Harry graduated from high school. She also recently realized that "the book that's being published is sort of the descendant of the book I started writing in a waiting room of a physical therapist's office when he was four." Though her journey with both her son and romance writing are anything but over, they both seem to have come pleasantly full circle. I end my telling here, but it's clear that things will continue to look up… actually, not unlike the ending of a romance novel.

Jillian Keegan is a Biomedical Engineering major.

Work Cited

"Romance Industry Statistics." *myRWA*. Romance Writers of America, 2013. Web. 6 Oct. 2013.

Profiles

CONSIDER THIS

- Like several other authors in this collection, Keegan utilizes "em dashes," a rhetorical choice that can bring some stylistic sophistication to an essay. As a form of punctuation, what purposes can em dashes serve? Do you incorporate them often—or at all—in your own writing?

- This essay discusses some of the conventions of the genre of writing known as "Romance," even referring to requirements that must be satisfied. With genre in mind, do you think the essay itself conforms to the conventions of the "profile genre"? In what ways might it deviate?

Fishing, Bears, and Wilderness Solitude:
Welcome to Battle River Wilderness Retreat

Sarah Conway

Reflective Memo: *I enjoyed writing this essay and found it very interesting to write. The process of interviewing my dad was special to me because I was able to hear his story and opinions of his job as a guide. I have followed in his footsteps and have become a guide as well, so it was neat to hear how he got started in the business. I love writing in a way that tells a story and someone can have a vivid picture of the scene in his or her head. While writing the profile essay, it was a little bit harder to do this. I was worried that I was doing too much "telling" of my dad's job instead of "showing" it. I struggled with this the most—setting up the essay in a way that the story would flow naturally. After interviewing my dad, I started the process of taking those answers and putting them into different sections and orders to make a story. I would write a paragraph usually around a quote, so it would be explained before and after. I really like the description in my essay, and I hope that readers can pic-ture themselves as guests at Battle River Wilderness Retreat, being guided by Tim Conway.*

The breeze starts to pick up as I cast my line into the rushing waters of the Battle River. My eyes follow the indicator tied on my line, as I wait for a rainbow trout to strike. There are so many red sockeye salmon crowding the river, it's almost impossible to spot the dark figure of a trout. As I patiently wait for a sudden tug on my line, I hear someone yell, "HEY BEAR!" and I turn to look. Fifty-yards downriver from me, a mighty grizzly bear comes crashing out of the alders and dives into the river, its eyes fixed on catching a sockeye salmon. As the rest of the guests frantically step back, watching this creature with both awe and fear, I look at our guide, who is only twenty-five yards from the bear. He quickly tells us to get back in the boat, but reassures us that the bear is more interested in catch-ing a meal than one of us. On our way back to camp, my mind replays the bear incident. I can't help but think that even in that situation, I have never doubted my safety or trust with Tim Conway as my guide. He does this routine every day and has over twenty-five years of experience as a fly-fishing and bear photography guide in the Southwestern wilderness of Alaska.

Tim grew up in the out-of-doors, but never learned to fly-fish until he came to Alaska. He grew up with a shotgun for hunting and a spinning rod for fishing. Just after he graduated from college, he and his best friend, John, decided that they would finally make one of their dreams come true and take a trip to the wil-derness of Alaska. While on their vacation, the two befriended the owner of Cry of the Loon Lodge who mentioned that he needed more help in guiding. Tim jumped at this wonderful opportunity and expressed his interest. However, when fishing the rivers of Alaska, it is mostly fly-fishing. The owner of Cry of the Loon

Lodge taught Tim how to fly-fish, and by the next summer, Tim was a licensed fishing guide managing the lodge.

After two summers of working at the lodge, Tim was becoming a little frustrated with his position and wanted more. "I was working for somebody else and didn't get to determine who came as guests, but I still took care of them," he says, "Some people who came to the lodge had been sold more than we had to offer and I had to deal with those issues and keep them happy. I had heard that Battle, a small, run down camp that hadn't been used in years might be available and knew that I could run my own camp. I would be able to establish the fishing program, book the guests and make my own decisions." It was just that simple. After talking to Sonny Petersen, owner of the multiple lodges in Katmai National Park including Battle, Tim worked out a deal to lease the camp which is now called Battle River Wilderness Retreat.

LOOK HERE

Watch amazing footage of bears in the Katmai National Park:

http://www.youtube.com/watch?v=ik-xss5BQKA

The huffing breath and stomping paws vibrate the ground. Only a wall separates the grizzly bear outside and Tim's cot. Suddenly, the walls of the cabin start to shake violently. Tim awakes to this familiar "earthquake." He knows that there is a bear having its morning backrub on the corner of the cabin, which just so happens to be where his pillow is. Tim lays in bed as he waits for the bear to move on its way through the rest of the camp. As it quiets down, Tim gets out of bed, puts on jeans, boots, and a fleece, and slowly opens the door to the outside. There's no sight of the bear, so he continues outside to the cookhouse. Along the way he yells "Hey Bear!" to make noise. One of the biggest safety rules at camp is to always make noise to let a bear know you're coming so you don't surprise them. When he reaches the cookhouse, he turns off the surrounding electric fence, and starts the coffee. It's about six o'clock in the morning.

Within the next hour, guests start to trickle in, wanting that first cup of hot coffee to wake them up. They are welcomed by an *Alabama* tape playing in the background and the smell of sizzling bacon cooking on the stove. Tim prepares breakfast every morning to serve about 7:00 A.M. By eight o'clock, all the guests head to their cabins and get dressed for a day downriver. Meanwhile, Tim does the breakfast dishes and starts on the next meal. While making sandwiches to pack for lunch, he glances at the ridge out the window and sees a sow with her spring-born cub trailing behind. He smiles as he finishes bagging up the last sandwich. He runs to the Crew Cabin to slip on his waders, grab the life vests, and then heads to the boat. He carefully loads all of the guests' fishing rods and cameras. As they float downriver, Tim carefully points out rainbow trout to those who can't spot them among the sea of red sockeye salmon. This is a skill he has perfected over many years of guiding. The river starts to pick up its pace and Tim is forced to get out of the boat and help the boat maneuver its way down through Boulder Dash. While the boat finds a path in between the boulders, a grizzly bear pops out of the alders, its nose sniffing in the air. The minute it smells the boat full of guests, it swings its head to see what's there. The bear photographers frantically scramble to get their cameras out. Tim knows that if the photographers can get that perfect picture, they will be happy and are more likely to return to Battle. He slows down the boat, enabling an opportunity for the photographers to snap a shot of this powerful creature. Tim lets out fishermen as he floats downriver to an island, where he lands the boat. The fishermen wade downriver and fish at the same time. Tim helps those who are just learning on the island and points out fish for them. Many lines tend to break, so quite a bit of his time is spent tying on hooks, beads, and more line. At about five o'clock in the afternoon, all of the guests are ready to go back to camp. Tim fires up the boat engine and takes his guests safely back upriver.

When back at camp, the guests shower and get warm, while Tim starts to prepare dinner. He throws steak on the outdoor barbeque and returns back inside to fix the salad. While chopping up the vegetables, he carefully watches the steak from the kitchen window, making sure a bear doesn't wander into camp, wanting a free meal. He sets all of the hot, prepared food on the checkered, cloth table at seven o'clock sharp. People from all over the country engage in conversation over a simple meal of steak, rice and salad. After dinner, Tim does the dishes and then takes out the trash. "Taking out the trash" at Battle means that you go to the Burn Barrel. Guests and guides stand around the barrel together, some sipping Jack Daniel's, all laughing and telling jokes. At about 9:30 when the burn is finished, Tim leads everyone back to the Cook Shack for a game of cards and dessert. This finishes off a typical day for Tim Conway as the head guide and operator of Battle River Wilderness Retreat.

Battle River is in an extremely remote location. No roads. No cell reception. No computers. No television. A camp like this offers a complete disconnect from the world. Tim loves this and finds it to be one of the many things that make Battle unique. "I would say that it is a wilderness solitude mixed with two incredible resources: trophy Rainbow Trout fishing, and brown bear photography," Tim gladly says. "There may be only a handful of camps in the world like Battle where you can see the bears so close and have great fishing as well." Tim allows guests to have the experience of a lifetime, but always in a safe way. He allows guests to get close up pictures of bears from the boat and cabins in camp. At many other camps and lodges, there are viewing platforms, which isn't as personal as the unique guided experience at Battle.

Tim enjoys being a guide and teaching people how to fish and showing them the way of the bears. However, sometimes being a guide and running a camp isn't always the easiest job. Tim says that, "The hardest part is probably dealing with the elements. You never know what the camp will be like when get there because it has been sitting there unattended for about ten months. Weather can certainly hamper a trip, and there are always unpredictability of bears and fishing. You have to have alternate plans when those things occur. Having to deal with the reaction of some guests to these elements can also be difficult." Although there can be tough parts when running a fishing and bear photography business, Tim ultimately enjoys being a guide and running Battle River Wilderness Retreat. He works hard through his long days, but he says it's worth it. "I love to fish, so I get to work and do something I love at the same time," he says with a smile, "I also love the wilderness and rustic nature of the camp. You are in such a remote area and the smallness of the camp makes it even better. I enjoy the isolation from technology and love sharing the atmosphere of Battle with people that appreciate it. That's what keeps me doing it. If people didn't appreciate it, then I couldn't afford to keep running it up there by myself."

Sarah Conway is an Agricultural Communications major.

CONSIDER THIS

- In her "Reflective Memo," the author discusses her concerns that she is "telling" the reader about her subject instead of "showing" the reader. Can you identify passages in which she might illustrate more of her subject's actions? Moreover, what informs *your* thought processes as you decide when to "show" and when to "tell"?

- The author incorporates space breaks—commonly referred to as "white space"—between the third and fourth paragraphs and again between the sixth and seventh paragraphs. Why do you think she's done this? How would the essay read differently without these breaks?

Big Hearts and Cold Snow

Megan Johnson

Reflective Memo: *This essay was constructed in order to inform the audience about a certain subculture. The subculture I chose was ski patroller. Writing this essay was actually very easy for me because I already knew so much about the subculture and, as I had an extremely knowledgeable interviewee, I was able to learn even more. As far as my writing process went, I first had an hour-long interview with my stepfather and, afterwards, the essay practically wrote itself. The only challenge I faced while writing this essay was organizing it in a manner that made sense; however, this was not hard to overcome. My favorite part about this essay is the anecdote at the beginning. I believe that it was an effective way to really capture the attention of my audience.*

Imagine a beautiful Saturday morning in the mountains: the air is crisp, the wind is at a minimum, and there is a light snowfall fluttering down from the clouds. You wake up with butterflies in your stomach in anticipation of the day ahead. You are going skiing. You and your family bundle up, pack a lunch, and head for the ski resort. Then, after the agonizing process of renting your skis and boots, finding a locker to put all of your belongings in, and buying your lift ticket, you are finally able to hit the slopes. The day gets off to a marvelous start, the conditions are perfect, and you are having an ideal ski day. Until one moment completely turns this around … Your ski hits an edge, and, before you know it, you're tumbling down the mountain. Your skis and poles go every which way until you finally come to a stop. The snow is nestled around your entire body, your head is throbbing with so much pain it seems unbearable, and you can't seem to move any of your limbs. The silence around you becomes deafening, and your panic level rises tenfold with every passing second. You are helpless, you are alone, and you are scared beyond belief. That is, until you see a bright red jacket with a big white cross on it coming to your rescue. You look up into the confident face of a ski patroller, and, in that moment, you know that everything is going to be okay.

Besides gracefully handling high-pressure situations like these, the main job of a ski patroller is to promote safety, help skiers in need, and endorse the ski resort in a positive light. Unlike your classic nine to five desk job, there is no typical day in the life of a ski patroller. One day could be completely free of any issues or accidents, and the next day could be absolute chaos. However, when it really comes down to it, the concept of what a ski patroller does is actually quite simple: they are the ambulances of the mountain. According to Chuck Kull, my stepfather and retired ski patroller of thirty-four years, "the idea is to take people hurt on the hill, console them, comfort them, and get them off the mountain so they can get the medical help they need" (Kull). Because skiing is such a risky sport, there is no doubt that accidents will happen. Ski patrollers are there to handle these accidents with professionalism, so that—after they get the appropriate medical attention—skiers will be willing and able to return to the mountain. Without the help of the ski patrol staff, skiing at a resort would be absolute madness. In the end, patrollers are just there to make sure that everyone stays safe and is able to enjoy the sport they love.

Obviously, the role of a ski patroller is extremely important, and the patrollers have to deal with challenging situations time and time again. They may have to calm down a frantic mother who has lost her child, they may have to help a scared skier down a difficult slope, or they may even have to deal with a death. This is not an easy job, which means that the ski patrollers have to go through extensive training. First, there is an initial ski check with the head of the ski patrol department to see if the patrollers are a strong enough to handle the many straining physical tasks of a patroller. In this test, they must go down the hardest and steepest slopes the resort has to offer, which, as I can say first-hand, is not an easy task by any means. Then, if you survive that, you have to take a forty to sixty hour course in outdoor emergency care. This course covers everything from the run-of-the-mill first aid and CPR to what to do in the event of an avalanche or a lost skier. Then, if that wasn't enough, you must put in countless hours of shadowing the current ski patrollers. Shadowing involves meticulously learning the dynamics of the mountain, participating in various mock accidents, and fine-tuning the imperative skills that were learned in the classroom. The time and effort put into just the training of a ski patroller is tremendous, and each patroller does it with a smile on their face—even though they aren't earning a dime (that's right, the training AND the job are unpaid).

As you can see, it takes a special type of person to become a ski patroller. Of course, there are a select few patrollers who are just in it for the free ski pass, but, for the most part, every patroller is there solely for the purpose of helping others. They have huge hearts, and are willing to do almost anything for one another and for distressed skiers. Chuck described his fellow ski patrollers in this way: "Most of us are compassionate, free-spirited, dedicated, family oriented, and in love with the sport of skiing" (Kull). Furthermore, once you've actually met with a dedicated ski patroller and seen them in action, it's easy to see that each of these adjectives is, in fact, extremely

LOOK HERE

To see ski patrollers in action, check out the short video, "Life of a Patroller":

http://youtu.be/uOO9ZGqpDwM

accurate. Patrollers have to be willing to give up their weekends in favor of working a ten to twelve hour day for free; they have to be able to devote the time and energy into strenuous training; they have to be prepared to give up skiing solely with their friends and family; they have to have the means to purchase their own skiing equipment, not for their own personal enjoyment, but to save the lives of others; most importantly, they have to be aware of the fact that they may not be able to save everyone that they try to save.

Skiing is a dangerous sport, and accidents can sometimes be fatal. With a huge sigh, Chuck mustered the words, "It pulls at my heartstrings; some people out there don't have mothers or brothers, or children, because we couldn't save them in time. You just wish you could have been there sooner, dug them up [from an avalanche] faster, or compressed their chest further. Watching someone breathe their last breath is something that you will never forget" (Kull). A ski patroller has to be strong, poised, and has to be prepared to look death right in the face. It's not an easy job, which begs the question: why? Why go through the training? Why devote the time and energy? Why willingly put yourself in a position so closely associated with hurting and fatality? I wondered the same thing, but Chuck had a simple answer: it was for that one time you do get there in time, for that one life that is saved. "I take pride in knowing that there are people out there that may not be here if I wasn't there when they needed me." (Kull).

Ski patrollers change lives. I have witnessed the sense of relief that a ski patroller brings to a distressed patient first hand. It is an overwhelming event to be a part of, and I can truly say that not many people would be able to handle everything ski patrollers do. As mentioned earlier, my stepfather was a ski patroller for thirty-four years. He has told me countless ski patrolling stories that really encompass the entire ski patrolling subculture; they demonstrate the hard work, dedication, compassion, and down-right bravery that every ski patroller seems to have in an overwhelming capacity. As I interviewed Chuck about his experience with ski patrolling, I could really feel the passion in his voice. When asked if he would do it all over again, he choked back tears and said, "…I wouldn't change it for anything. If my physical ability would allow me to do this longer, I would. Other than raising my four children, there has been nothing more rewarding in my life" (Kull). There is no question that patrollers are an extraordinary group of people, and I cannot even begin to explain how proud I am to say that I was raised by one.

Megan Johnson is a Business Administration major.

Work Cited

Kull, Chuck. Personal interview. 19 April 2014.

CONSIDER THIS

- You may find that your essays gain rhetorical strength through variation in both paragraphing and sentence structure. This author tends to follow a somewhat repetitive form in which she uses a similar construction in successive sentences. How might this essay change if she moved toward a more varied composition?

- Though Johnson profiles her stepfather, she uses his experience to comment on the vocation of ski patroller in a more general sense. How does her stepfather's experience work to support her overall definition of the vocation?

Wild Child

Dylan Grant

Reflective Memo: *In this essay, I describe the accomplishments of my personal friend Tanner Saul. In high school, he did extensive work with the National Park Service on a case study concerning mountain lions in the local area. He also conducted his own study comparing the presence of wildlife in an urban area versus a rural area. I contacted him via text and then conducted an interview through FaceTime. From there I wrote my rough draft, in which I included as many details as I could. When I needed some additional information I would text Tanner. My rough draft ended up mediocre. I felt there were a lot of stylistic errors as well as underdeveloped descriptions. So I went back, got a couple more details from Tanner, as well as some of the emotions he felt during each stage in his adventures. I elongated some of my descriptions and tried to include some personal reactions to some of the work he did. I think my final draft is much stronger. It feels more emotional and flows better than the rough draft did. I think the strengths of the essay definitely lie in the descriptions of his ventures and also the idea of how unique his situation was. I think the weaknesses of the essay are some of the transitions as well as the description of the emotion involved in his work. Every time he would tell me about something in high school I was always left in shock that he was already this deep into a career, but it was tough to convey that kind of reaction on paper.*

"Two roads diverged in a wood and I—I took the one less traveled by, and that has made all the difference."   —Robert Frost

Tanner Saul was not the typical high school student. While many kids were trying to excel at sports or studying for their next test, Tanner was out in the Santa Monica Mountains, tracking mountain lions. Instead of just going to class like everybody else, he involved himself in a mountain lion study with the National Park Service. This study involved preserving the endangered mountain lion species in the Santa Monica and Santa Susana Mountains, as well as Griffith Park. "They are in danger of disappearing from these areas because it is an island of habitat that is surrounded by urban development and major freeways. This puts them in danger of inbreeding—which has already started to take place—and eventually may lead to sterile individuals not allowing for the generation to continue unless these lions are able to crossbreed with lions from other areas with different genetic codes to help sustain the population." Not many people get the chance or have the ability to go down such a unique path. Of course, he didn't just end up there. He had an interest in something, and through countless hours out in the wild and huge amounts of effort and entrepreneurship, he was able to turn that interest into a promising career path. He is a role model for anyone pursuing a goal or passion.

Ever since I have known Tanner—about ten years—he has been above average. The most notable feature about him has always been his observational prowess. I remember one instance when we were skiing together. We were waiting in line for the ski lift and he points to what I thought was a random stranger and says, "That guy was sitting at the table across from us yesterday." That dropped my jaw. Another time, I was hiking with Tanner. Every once in a while he would point to the ground, claiming to see a bear track or a coyote track or a deer track. I would sometimes have to get down on my hands and knees to verify the print was actually there, but he was always right. That observational skill alone did not get him to tracking mountain lions, however. He always had an admirable adoration for the outdoors and a love for animals. He lived right next to the Santa Monica Mountains, so he could often be found hiking, fishing, or trying to build a fort out of dead trees. It was obvious that he wasn't bound for a traditional career.

His path really started to diverge when he purchased a trail camera to observe the wildlife around his home. At first, all he saw were coyotes, deer, and rabbits; but after about six months, he came upon something amazing: a mountain lion had walked past his camera. "When I first saw the puma my heart stopped and I couldn't breathe. I knew that was a moment that would stay with me for the rest of my life." But there was something peculiar about the lion. Around its neck it wore a collar, and in its ear hung a tag. Curious as to the origin of the devices, he uploaded the video to YouTube asking if anyone knew anything about it. In just a few hours, he received a reply from the lead biologist on a study concerning the mountain lions in that area. He was told that the collar was a GPS tracking device, and that it had malfunctioned. To say this was exciting for Tanner is an understatement. Not only had he seen a lion, but he was being contacted by a professional in the field of wildlife. He had found a passion. Thus, his career as a tracker began.

For about a year and a half, Tanner would occasionally be in contact with the head biologist on the study, Jeff Sikich. Every once in a while he would accompany Sikich in tracking a mountain lion. These ventures were necessary because the collars often malfunctioned and he had to regularly check on the health of the lions. After that time, he developed a better relationship with Sikich, and

LOOK HERE

Read more about mountain lions in the Santa Monica Mountains here:

http://friendsofgriffithpark.org/ article-bigCat.php

Discover ways that *you* can get involved with California wildlife:

http://www.nwfcalifornia.org

became a more active participant in the study. He began going out with Sikich more often, going on treks that could last all day or all night. He would often have a story that began with "I went out tracking at 2 AM last night and didn't get home until 8 AM." The commitment he showed to assisting in this study was astounding. Keep in mind he was not paid during this time. He was volunteering countless hours just to do something that he wanted to do.

As Tanner became increasingly involved in this study, he devoted less time to other aspects, such as schoolwork. Some would consider this a mistake, or at least the traditionalists would say so. However, Tanner was not depriving himself of any learning experience. He was taking his education outside the classroom. "Sometimes I would get a call from the biologist during class, and I wouldn't care—I would just step outside and take the call." Obviously, his priorities were not the same as many other students. However, many other students did not have the same kind of passion that Tanner had.

Over time, Tanner developed a deeper understanding of wildlife and the interactions between man and animal. From working with Sikich, he learned how to track and capture animals. This was necessary to repair malfunctioned collars or take blood samples from the mountain lions. When considering the level of skill and knowledge one must have to go out and track mountain lions, it is impressive that Tanner could participate so actively. Often, he would go tracking with the head biologist and a couple other interns. These interns were not high school age however. These were college graduates trying to get experience in the field. There was even a time when Tanner was asked to educate a classroom of UCLA students about the study because he was so knowledgeable about it. He describes his feelings about how he integrated himself into this select group of scientists. "As I worked my way up in the study I finally started to feel accepted in the small community of wildlife biologists." Tanner knew what he wanted. By following his own goals rather than the typical high school agenda, he was able to find something that interests him and pursue it at a much earlier time than most people.

Going into Tanner's senior year in high school, he decided to extend his education even further. Along with continuing to participate in the mountain lion study, he began his own study. He monitored the presence of wildlife in a rural environment and in an urban environment in order to see where wildlife was more prolific. On his own time, he set up two trail cameras, one in Verdugos and one in the San Gabriel Mountains. He recorded all of the data by himself and only required assistance when writing the case report. This study was done over a period of three months and some interesting results were found. He found that there were a surprising number of mountain lions active in the urban area. Also, there were a lot of bobcats active during the day, which contradicted many other studies showing bobcats are often only active at night. This case study was a big step for his career and was very important for his own reasons. "Starting my own study made me feel more independent and in control over how I wanted the study set up." This was not like any project in school. He was gaining real experience doing something of his own accord. For his entrepreneurship, he was awarded the Young Naturalist Award, a prestigious award given to students who show significant participation and communication in science. The excitement in being recognized for all the hard work was enormous, "I actually screamed on the phone!" He traveled to New York to participate in an awards ceremony. He followed his passion, and because of the effort and time he put into all of it, he was well recognized.

Today, Tanner is continuing his education at the University of Montana, majoring in Wildlife Biology. He chose this school because it offers this specific major. He aspires to become a lead biologist of his own study, preferably concerning large felines. Obviously, he is already well on his way to achieving that. While many students Tanner's age are still trying to figure out what they want to study in college, he has been working on his career for three years already. He started with an interest, developed that interest into a passion, and will hopefully enjoy a fulfilling career.

Dylan Grant is an Electrical Engineering major.

CONSIDER THIS

- This essay begins with an epigraph by Robert Frost. How are epigraphs different from other quotations featured in an essay? And what function or functions do epigraphs serve? How does the Frost epigraph frame Grant's essay?

- Grant states that his subject, Tanner Saul, "is a role model for anyone pursuing a goal or passion." As a writer, do you have role models that you look to for guidance or inspiration? Are there certain modes or styles of writing that you have emulated in the past or would like to emulate in the future?

- In his "Reflective Memo," the author mentions that he "tried to include some personal reactions" on his subject's work. Can you identify these moments of personal reaction? How would the essay change if such moments were handled differently, or even left out altogether?

Where is Home?

Katie Miyoshi

Reflective Memo: *I wrote this essay in hopes of both exploring and introducing the idea of a growing population of TCKs (Third Culture Kid). Being a TCK myself, I felt a personal connection when researching and writing this essay. I was also able to use my own experiences in this essay, thus building my ethos and pathos. Perhaps one challenge that I faced was the difficulty in bringing in logos through the factual evidence in my sources. Creating a flowing essay with a voice was difficult. I really enjoyed writing on this topic.*

"So, where are you from?"

The group of freshly admitted college students stared and waited for my response. A few eyebrow raises and giggles. The circle we were sitting in no longer felt like Dexter Lawn. It felt like a vortex of embarrassment and confusion. For a few seconds, I sat and thought. It was a question I did not know how to answer. A question I am still unable to answer.

"San Diego. San Jose. San Luis Obispo."

Everyone answered. Brief answers. Simple. As for me, the answer is not so simple. Born to a Filipino mother and a third generation Japanese father in Los Angeles, things were already complicated to explain. It gets worse. After living in Los Angeles for a large chunk of my life, I moved to Tokyo. Now living in San Luis Obispo. Where is home? Why am I so uncertain, and why does my answer have to be a repetitive, elaborate rant? "Week of Welcome" should not have been so unwelcoming. I felt lost.

With improvements in technology and transportation, the world is becoming increasingly globalized, and with this crossbreeding of cultures comes a growing population of "lost" children termed, "TCK." Third Culture Kid. The term was coined by John and Ruth Useem in the 1960s, defining "first culture to be the non-Western culture in which an individual was living, the second culture as the American culture, and the third culture as the behavior patterns created, shared, and learned by men of different societies who are in the process of relating their societies, or portions thereof, to each other" (qtd. in Bonebright). Later, this term became more generalized and expanded to include all cross-cultured individuals lacking a single culture they can call their own.

It is often thought that this population of "TCKs" is rare and a unique occurrence. Yet, one could not be more wrong. My first day at Yokohama International School, I discovered a brand new world. It was a hybrid of varying cultures working, living, and schooling together. I befriended a tall, blonde Dutch girl who had just recently lived in Beijing. I met a German boy who lived in Russia, Hong Kong, and New York. I sat next to a South African girl who lived equally between

Montana and Tokyo. Every one of these children had the unfortunate inability to identify home, and I was one of them.

Despite the tiresome explanations, there are advantages and disadvantages to growing up amongst a variation of cultures. Such experiences not only alter a child's perspective toward becoming more global, but they also have social, psychological, and intellectual consequences. Thus these experiences become much more influential throughout the TCK's entire life.

Perhaps one of the most substantial effects of being a TCK is on his or her social understanding and behaviors. For many, change can be stressful and foreboding, but the TCK welcomes such change and demonstrates extrovert attitudes in response. One TCK describes his experiences in international school and explains, "You get kind of used to the system of constant change and meeting new people and being forced to understand different people's experiences, but at the same time joining together to build an experience together" (Premack). Through constant movement and understanding of varying cultures, TCKs are able to understand cultural subtleties and develop their social skills. Shyness is not an option when constantly required to make new friends.

Yet, even with such exceptional social skills, there is a drawback in the social aspect of community acceptance and assimilation. Being half Japanese and having lived there for a couple years, some people believe that it would be easier for me to understand the culture; however,

> **LOOK HERE**
>
> Adrian Bautista presents the experience of several "Third Culture Kids" in her short documentary, *So Where's Home?*:
> **http://vimeo.com/41264088**

in actuality this is not the case. The subtle hints of my darker skin, American accent, and even the way I dress, spotlight my distinct differences against the Japanese background society. In the video, "So Where's Home?" Amy Burns, a Korean blooded, Tokyo and American bred student describes, "I never felt like a local despite the fact that I lived there from when I was 5 until right before college. I was always a foreigner" (Bautista). One can live in a country for years and learn the culture; however, being born with a different look or blood will always indicate dissimilarity and, therefore, exclusion.

Although rootless, being a TCK does have its benefits as far as education and knowledge go. According to a peer-reviewed scholarly journal, "Adult TCKs participate in higher education at a very high rate" (Bonebright). This is partially due to the likelihood of their successful expatriate parents having a higher education and attending quality international schools. With a combination of a high quality education, traveling experience, and multilingualism, TCKs are ideal for universities and multinational corporations.

With the numerous economic and intellectual benefactors that accompany being a TCK, there are also emotional and psychological consequences that accompany a life of constant transition and ever-changing environments. Journalist Nina Sichel, who studies TCKs, identifies the troubling side of this nomadic lifestyle by coining another term, "TCK grief," which has similar symptoms to depression or post-traumatic stress. This depression and stress stems from grief of loss:

> The layers of loss run deep: Friends, community, pets. Family, toys, language. Weather, food, culture. Loss of identity. Loss of a place of comfort, stability, a safe and predictable world. Home. These children are losing the worlds they love, over and over. They cycle through the stages of grief each time they move—or they don't, and push it down, submerge it, only to have it bubble up later in life, unexplained. (Sichel)

Perhaps it is not just frustration that lies in the question, "Where is home?" There is a loss of identity, which is disconcerting for children and even adults. The question becomes, "Who am I?" And this particular question is much more daunting. A lack of a grounding element begs us to question our values and constantly alter our feelings.

TCKs are the global citizens, belonging nowhere and everywhere at the same time. Sometimes they feel "most at home at the airport" (Bautista). Sometimes they identify with more than one country as home. Yet, despite the benefits and drawbacks, TCKs have the opportunity to adapt the parts of cultures they identify with and reject those that do not appeal to them. It is this development and fusion that creates the Third Culture Kid. A group of "lost" children, unsure of their origins and cultures. A classification becoming more universally taken and known in the contemporary world. They are a flourishing generation washing away the lines of disparity and cultural segregation. With that, there is no identification to connect with "home." Therefore the question, "Where are you from?" is rendered useless. We are left with:

"Who are you? What is your story?"

Katie Miyoshi is an Architecture major.

Works Cited

Bautista, Adrian. *So Where's Home?: A Film About Third Culture Kid Identity.* 2012. Online video clip. Vimeo. 19 February 2014.

Bonebright, Denise. "Adult Third Culture Kids: HRD Challenges and Opportunities." *Human Resource Development International* 13.3 (2010): 351–9. Print.

Premack, Rachel. "The Third Culture Kid: Between Homelands." *The Michigan Daily* 10 February 2014. Print.

Sichel, Nina. "The Trouble with Third Culture Kids." *Morning Zen.* Web. 19 February 2014.

CONSIDER THIS

- In this essay, Miyoshi uses her own experience as a "Third Culture Kid" to enhance and explain the subject of her essay. Does her anecdote succeed in getting you interested in her argument?

- The writer inserts, on two separate occasions, long quotes from her sources that respectively define the term "Third Culture Kid" and offer a glimpse at the physical and mental side effects these individuals experience. Generally, it's important for a writer to take some space following each quote to analyze or explain it at length. Does the writer effectively connect her use of the definition to her surrounding text?

Defying Gender Roles with Friendship and Ponies

Liam Gow

Reflective Memo: *This essay was very enjoyable to write. As I was already familiar with the subject, writing about it came easily and was fun as well. The flipside,
however, was that it became hard to sort the wheat from the chaff when it came to
informing the reader. My subject was esoteric enough that a decent background was
necessary to discuss it much, but on the other hand, this wasn't writing intended just
to inform. Balancing the types of content was a big challenge in this essay, but in the
end I found that there were a fair number of points that I could make implicitly in
the information and then draw upon thereafter. Of the essays I wrote for English 134,
I liked this one the best. It gave me a chance to put more of myself—of my style—
into it, and as a result it is closer to my heart.*

If you've visited the Internet much in the last couple years, you might have
noticed a growing saturation of images of pastel-colored ponies. If you watch
the news, you might have seen shock stories of grown men liking little girls' TV
shows. If you live in a big city, you might have seen swarms of teens and twenty-
somethings in brightly colored costumes. If you know what I'm talking about,
then the Brony subculture has already reached you. If not, allow me to explain:
Bronies, an amalgamation of the words "Bro" and "Pony" are teen and adult fans
of the TV show *My Little Pony: Friendship is Magic* (*MLP:FiM* hereafter). The
obvious question is why. The reasons generally cited by Bronies for watching this
show are the good quality of animation, voice acting, and most importantly, plot.
It's just a nice, wholesome show that anyone, not just little girls, can enjoy.

The Brony fandom originated on 4chan—an infamous forum widely
regarded as the most disturbed (and disturbing) place on the Internet. They saw
the show and appreciated the funny writing, good voice acting, and enjoyable art
style. Needless to say, they were surprised and horrified. However, the denizens of
4chan, generally speaking, are pretty devoid of conscience. Though their mascu-
line pride was offended, the collective atmosphere of the image board and lack of
inhibitions caused by Internet anonymity meant that many continued to watch
the show regardless of the fact that it was *My Little Pony*.

Despite the negative connotations of femininity and childishness, the popularity of the show quickly skyrocketed, taking over discussions on other areas
of 4chan, as these new Bronies spread the word. 4chan eventually banned pony
related content on its boards to prevent the spam. While many Bronies did leave
4chan for less hostile websites, many continued regardless, and in the end the
ban was lifted with the condition that pony-related content would be kept to the
newly created /mlp/ board. By this point, however, the exodus of Bronies from

4chan's ban had already seen many sites either develop a Brony presence or whole new sites created to house pony-related content. The 4chan era had ended, and Bronies were now unleashed on the Internet as a whole. Without the 4chan ban, the fandom would likely have stayed there, and not spread out as it did.

To gain a greater understanding of Bronies on a more personal level, I interviewed Alton DeHaan. He's been a Brony since November 2011, and co-founded the Cal Poly Bronies and Pegasisters Club. The first meeting attracted thirty-five students, and attendance has remained more or less constant since. Initially, the club just showed new episodes when they aired, but over time, has evolved into "a really great network of friends at Cal Poly." They continue to meet, watch old episodes and fandom content, and hang out even when the show isn't airing.

As Bronies became more well known on the Internet, they started to attract attention from the mainstream media. This attention has been mixed to negative. Fox News, especially, has run several sensationalistic stories on the subject of Bronies, comparing them to terrorists and labeling the trend "stupid and unbelievably ridiculous." At the heart of the matter is the preconception that men should like "manly" things: sports; violent video games; beer. Not pastel ponies and happiness. There is an assumption in common society that *My Little Pony* is inherently poor, and that only homosexuals or sexual deviants would want to watch it. Lauren Faust, the show's creator, articulates the struggle of the Bronies:

> As a group, they have not succumbed to society's pressure that young men must hold contempt for anything feminine no matter what. They've been able to see beyond the preconceived notions that they were most likely raised with to judge something for it's [sic] merit. And on top of that, they're brave enough to embrace it openly despite the ridicule that they are undoubtedly subject to.

By refusing to be limited by existent definitions of acceptable behavior, Bronies can induce real change.

More and more, normal people are being shown that Bronies aren't necessarily perverts or pedophiles, just because they like a show aimed at little girls. In an effort to show Bronies in a more positive light, Brony charities have been set up, and have raised hundreds of thousands of dollars. John de Lancie, who voices the character Discord in the show, has created a documentary about Bronies aimed at the general public, providing a third-party angle on Bronies' harmlessness and portraying the sympathetic perspective on the discrimination Bronies face. Most recently, the movie *Equestria Girls* meant that Bronies and

LOOK HERE

Get a glimpse of the Brony culture with this trailer for director John de Lancie's documentary:

http://youtu.be/ohnuyqJyEW0

normal families met in person. Alton is of the opinion that the exposure has increased awareness and made the fandom more mainstream. Overall, he feels that being a Brony has "become so common that it's no longer a niche thing."

Alton defines a Brony as "anyone that's a fan of the show," and by all estimates, that number is still growing. The fourth season of *MLP:FiM* will be airing soon, and *Equestria Girls* did better than expected. A recent study, Brony Herd Census, estimates with 95% confidence somewhere between 7 and 12 million people who strongly identify as Bronies in the US Internet-using community alone, equating to approximately one twentieth of the total population of the United States. To use Alton's broader definition, there may be as many as 30 million in the US alone. With this sort of power of numbers behind them, and as more people are exposed to them in positive ways, they have the potential to influence societal change. Joe Kilmartin, "manager of Toronto's Comic Book Lounge and Gallery," is hopeful:

> I think the definition of what it means to be a man is unfortunately still what it was 50 years ago, but this is a signal that things are ready to change. If it doesn't happen immediately, it's going to happen in generations after ours because if it's something as casual as this, it says a lot about where things will go. It's a signal that those old tropes about what it means to be a man, and the things you can like as a guy, are falling away.

If this is true, more than ever, it is important to understand how the Brony phenomenon will continue into the future: will it bring about this prophesized social change, leading the way for the breakdown of gender stereotypes, or will it disappear, leaving only a shrunken group of fanatics behind? When I asked Alton where he thought the fandom was headed, he told me that "The only thing that will stop the fandom is the show ending." It might take couple of years, but "it would eventually go away." The crux of his prediction is new content. Without it, he says, a "fandom dries up."

Personally, I have a more optimistic view. I have seen only a small section of the colossal number of memes and fan-works that the fandom has made, but if anything, production increases when the show isn't airing. Fan-works create more fan-works, building off the creativity of the community. Whole continuities or genres build off a single story, like with *The Conversion Bureau* and *Fallout: Equestria*, which have each spawned dozens of stories and millions of words. Fan-made episodes like *Snowdrop* create fan-favorite characters. It seems to me that many parts of the fandom have almost cut ties to the show and are now exploring their own creations. New people are being introduced to the fandom and its creations all the time. The durability of the original 4chan'ers lives on in the Bronies of the present: adaptable, welcoming, and ever expanding. Even if the show is cancelled, I think that the fandom will live on.

I chose to examine Bronies as a trend because of the positive traits they embody by breaking free of gender roles. While there has been a great deal of freedom of expression for women, men's gender roles have remained largely stagnant, as evidenced by the massive controversy surrounding Bronies. My primary aim was to understand whether the *MLP:FiM* fandom has a future, so that it might continue to pioneer the challenging of gender roles. My findings have been mixed. While Alton doubts the long-term pervasiveness of the fandom, I have seen the activity that the community is capable of, even when the show is not airing. The amazing strength that the Brony fandom has so far demonstrated through 4chan, internet, and mainstream media criticism shows me that there is hope that they may be able to overcome future obstacles as well and bring about the societal change that is so tantalizingly close.

Liam Gow is an Electrical Engineering major.

Works Cited

4chan. 4chan, 3 Nov 2013. Web. 3 Nov. 2013.

Barnes, Mike. "Shout Factory, Hasbro in Deal for More 'My Little Pony' (Exclusive)." *The Hollywood Reporter.* The Hollywood Reporter, 13 Aug. 2013. Web. 3 Nov. 2013.

Bronies: The Extremely Unexpected Adult Fans of My Little Pony. Dir. Laurent Malaquais. Perf. John de Lancie. BronyDoc LLC, 2013. Film.

"CoderBrony." "My Little Pony: Statistics are Magic." Survey Monkey, 2013. Web. 3 Nov. 2013. DeHaan, Alton. Personal Interview. 25 Oct. 2013.

Faust, Lauren "fyre-flye." Comment. *deviantART.* deviantART, 7 Feb. 2012. Web. 3 Nov. 2013.

"FOX Attacks Bronies." *YouTube.* YouTube, 17 Jun 2011. Web. 3 Nov. 2013.

Hasbro. "My Little Pony: Friendship is Magic Logo." Wikipedia, 5 Aug. 2011. Web. 3 Nov. 2013.

"Just a Little Quick Math with Brony Charities." *Bronies For The Better.* Tumblr, 8 Aug 2012. Web. 3 Nov. 2013.

Kilmartin, Joe. "'My Little Pony' Not Just For Girls Anymore: Meet The Bronies." Interview by Aaron Broverman. *Huffpost TV.* TheHuffingtonPost.com Inc., 23 Oct. 2012. Web. 3 Nov. 2013.

"My Little Pony: Friendship is Magic." *Hub Television Network LLC.* Hasbro, 10 Oct. 2010.

"My Little Pony Friendship is Magic: Season 4 Promo." *YouTube.* YouTube, 26 Oct. 2013. Web. 3 Nov. 2013.

"RedEye on Bronies." *YouTube.* YouTube, 17 Jun 2011. Web. 3 Nov. 2013.

"The Growing Trend of My Little Pony on 4chan." Chart. *Know Your Meme.* Cheezburger Inc., 6 Feb. 2011. Web. 3 Nov. 2013.

CONSIDER THIS

- How would you characterize the author's stance toward his subject? Does the author's position affect your perception of his profile subject?

- Generally, profile essays don't cite as many sources as are featured in this essay, and yet research can certainly be incorporated into profiles to great effect. As Gow mentions in his "Reflective Memo," profile writing isn't writing "just to inform." What else do you think a profile can or should do? What role could research play in a profile that you might write?

Public Rhetoric

*Which issues do you care most about? How can you use
rhetorical skills to effect change in the world?*

The authors featured in this section develop complex arguments about issues they care about, without leaving behind the perspectives of readers who may disagree with them. You may find that the more invested you become in the topics you write about, the stronger your writing becomes. Moreover, learning how to use *ethos*, *pathos*, and *logos* effectively will make you a greater rhetorician, writer, and thinker.

CONSIDER THIS

Signs of SLO

- Arguments really are everywhere. For instance, each of the signs on the following page from downtown SLO makes a claim about a specific space, location, or social issue. What claims are they making? Can you analyze these signs and tease the argument out of them? For instance, if a store displays a "buy local" sticker in its window, what is that store telling you about its approach to merchandise? Why is buying local important? What is the store's *ethos*?

- In addition, captions affect how we read images. What captions would you provide for the images to guide readers to interpret the signs in a particular way? When assembled together, do the signs make any claims about the San Luis Obispo community?

The "I Bike SLO County" image has been printed with permission of the San Luis Obispo Bicycle Coalition. All other photographs were taken by Brenda Helmbrecht.

Fed Up

Lauren Goette

Frequent illness, poor academic performance, lowered immune system, and depression: what do these things have in common? They are all linked to a lack of nutritious food. The pitiful state of Cal Poly's dining program is something that is widely acknowledged by students, but largely ignored by the school's dining administration. For a school that claims to care about the health of its students, the lack of wholesome food is astonishing. After seeing firsthand how the current dining system has negatively impacted my life and the lives of my peers, I can only say that we must demand a change. When the normal reaction to the mention of campus food is a grimace, we must demand a change. When the mental and physical health of students is put at risk, we must demand a change. It is time for Cal Poly to stop ignoring one of its largest issues. And no, this issue doesn't involve party rules or Greek life controversies. It is something so simple, yet so crucial to the success of the university and its students. If indeed, "you are what you eat," then Cal Poly's students are in trouble. In order to ensure the cultivation of healthy, happy, and successful students, it is imperative that Cal Poly step up and make numerous essential improvements to the horrid state of campus dining its students are forced to endure.

One of the many speculated improvements that should unquestionably be made is the addition of nutrition labels to all dining areas. According to an article in Cal Poly's newspaper, *Mustang Daily*, "The nutrition keys developed by Campus Dining consist of calorie content, saturated fat, sodium, sugars, protein and total carbohydrates" ("Fine"). Adding these labels will not only inform students about what they're eating, but it will also make it easier for them to make healthy choices if they so desire. With many of the food options containing high amounts of sodium, carbs, fat, or sugar, having a guide to dictate which foods to avoid and which to indulge in can be enormously helpful to students looking to avoid gaining the "freshman 15."

The addition of these facts is undoubtedly a step in the right direction; however, not everyone at Campus Dining is convinced that displaying nutritional information will significantly influence students' choices. Mike Thorton, director of Campus Dining, stated, "People believe that we should tell you what to eat, but that's not what we are here for" ("Fine"). Where Thorton is mistaken is his assumption that, in providing nutritional information to students, Campus Dining must undertake the daunting task of trying to force students to eat healthy. Although it would clearly be impossible to force students who eat on campus to make healthy choices, adding nutritional information does provide students with

a push in a healthier direction. Exactly how far does it push students? A 2006 study published by *The Journal of American College Health* put that question to the test. Their objective was to examine "when, why, if, and how nutrition labels impact food purchase decisions of college students" (Kolodinsky). To do this, the study monitored the daily food purchases of 110 students at on-campus dining and food outlets at a large northeastern university. When examining the purchases of the students, they found that "the label users, male and female, believed in the importance of having nutrition facts on food labels, whereas nonusers did not" (Kolodinsky). Yet, this did not mean that the only people using the information were solely health-conscious. The results also revealed that both "college women and men were interested in the provision of nutrition labels in the food court… and that those exposed to labels over the course of the study noticed the labels and often referred to them when making purchase decisions" (Kolodinsky).

This study paints a vivid picture of exactly how much nutrition facts can influence students' food purchases. Not only did the availability of the information help guide people already concerned with nutrition, it also influenced the buying decisions of people who normally would not consider the nutritional information of their food. In all, this study reveals that most students do care about the nutritional value of their food, and given the chance, they would choose a healthier option if one was labeled as such. Although there is talk of more positive dining changes like this at Cal Poly, many of them have yet to be seen. When it comes down to it, countless more improvements are necessary before the dining program can reach the quality its students deserve.

Another much-needed enhancement of Cal Poly's campus dining situation is the addition of a variety of choices for people with food intolerances or special diets. These options will make it significantly easier for people with dietary restrictions to get vital nutrients. When asked by *Mustang News* about the dining options available to people with allergies, student Lauren Matthews replied, "Many students on campus who have special dietary needs do not have sufficient options on campus, [and] the ones that are offered are minimal" ("Fine"). Being a vegan, this extreme lack of options has caused me more stress in this past quarter than I ever could have imagined. With few protein-rich entrees available, I (and, inevitably, my mother) dealt with the fear that I was not getting the protein, healthy fats, and assortment of fruits and veg-

LOOK HERE

Want to voice your concerns about campus dining? Find out how:

http://mustangnews.net/student-affairs-to-take-leadership-role-in-changing-campus-dining/

etables I needed. After my first few months as a freshman, I made the shocking discovery that I had been progressively losing weight since moving in in late

September. By November 2013, I had lost eight pounds, making me four pounds underweight. It was then that I realized just how nutritionally starved I was. The combination of the lack of nutrient-dense foods and the school-related stress I was experiencing ended up making me frequently ill. My illness reached its peak when I made an unexpected trip to the ER in January for symptoms of meningitis. At the hospital I discovered that I had lymphadenitis: a bacterial infection in the lymph nodes. As explained by my doctor, this infection was brought on by my weakened immune system. The disabling of my immune system, however, was not simply chance. Dr. Janet McElhaney, a geriatrician at the University of Connecticut Health Center in Farmington, stated there is strong evidence to show that "a well-balanced diet is a key to a stronger immune system… Of particular concern…is protein, because it has a direct effect on the blood cells in the body that fight infection" (Condon). Having experienced a weakened immune system myself directly after coming to Cal Poly, I can't help but feel that it was largely due to the scant variety of vegan protein sources. Although Campus Dining claims that "at most restaurants and markets on campus you can find foods that are dairy-free, gluten-free, vegetarian and even some vegan," the ratio of vegan food to non-vegan food is incredibly skewed ("Fine"). The only vegan sources of protein offered on campus are highly processed veggie burgers, canned beans, and tofu, whereas the meat offered has included cod, salmon, pork, steak, turkey, chicken, and even shark. By failing to provide adequate alternative sources of protein for vegetarians and vegans, Campus Dining is putting the immune health of these students at risk.

While students with special dietary cases struggle to find acceptable dining options, the entirety of Cal Poly's dining population is also faced with an even more concerning issue: the pitiable quality of the food. Numerous students have voiced complaints that the quality and preparation of campus food is not up to par. For instance, in early January 2014, freshman Theodore Tan posted a picture of his bloody lump of "rare" meat on Facebook. The photo, captioned "Gourmet extra rare meat courtesy of Metro," (referring to the campus restaurant 19 Metro Station), gained so much attention from peers that it caught the eye of *Mustang News* (McMinn). After Tan's story was published, *Mustang News* received an email from Cal Poly Corporation spokesperson Yukie Murphy, which stated, "Customers can request that their meat be served rare, medium, or well done—however they would like it" (McMinn). When Tan was interviewed about the photo, he replied, "There's rare steaks, then

LOOK HERE

See Tan's picture here:

http://mustangnews.net/facebook-photo-claims-too-show-way-to-rare-campus-dining-meat/

there's more than rare… It's like the inside was basically not cooked at all" (McMinn). This unsettling situation is just one of many instances where campus food has been criticized for being far less than desirable.

Despite students' outrage, however, it looks like the quality of food is doomed to stay the same. Campus Dining appears to be completely apathetic to the complaints of students, with its director stating, "We tend to get people who complain… Sometimes I just think that it's considered trendy to complain" ("Fine"). What Campus Dining seems to lack is a sense of exactly how much its customers are dissatisfied. What will it take for them to realize that these complaints aren't just "trendy"? What will it take for them to realize that these complaints are coming directly from the unnerving experiences students continue to have with their food? No matter how much students protest, Campus Dining continues to turn a blind eye to its problems. Another example of Campus Dining's venality can be seen in Thorton's response to students choosing a well-known fast-food restaurant on campus over Campus Dining eateries. In an interview with *Mustang News*, Thorton commented, "You make a choice to go get a taco or Chick-fil-A… There are tempting things, but it is our job to provide the things that consumers desire… If the people did not want the food, they wouldn't buy it, and we wouldn't continue to offer it" ("Fine"). But what if the rest of campus food was so poor you felt like you had no choice but to resort to Chick-fil-A on a daily basis? That's exactly the situation that students like Evan De La Huerta find themselves in every day. According to De La Huerta, "if the food looked better, I would try it … but I just don't trust it" ("Fine"). As a result, De La Huerta opts for a Chick-fil-A sandwich and fries, one of the highest calorie meals on campus when combined with a beverage. Still, De La Huerta's skepticism about the food is understandable. Annie Faller, a food science major, who is required to work in multiple Campus Dining restaurants as a lab for class, told *Mustang News* that not all of the food used by Campus Dining is fresh. In fact, she admitted, "There is a lot of canned, processed food" ("Fine"). For Campus Dining, the use of processed foods is viewed as cost-effective. But while they're decreasing costs, they're subsequently decreasing the physical and mental health of Cal Poly students.

Yet, Campus Dining does have the power to lead its customers to success where it is currently failing them. One study conducted by the Mental Health Foundation "suggests diet could have an immediate and lasting effect on mental health. It links changes in the human diet over the past 60 years, such as increased consumption of processed food… with the country's worsening mental health" (Brody). This shocking connection realized by a number of mental health officials is just the tip of the iceberg when it comes to the positive effects good nutrition can have on the mind. In addition to a boost in mental health, "recent studies by the Centers for Disease Control and Prevention… have found a strong

link between nutrition…and academic performance. Student health has a direct impact on cognitive skills and attitudes toward academic behavior, and results in better concentration" (Kochakian). When Campus Dining provides its customers with such low-quality, high-processed food, they are depriving students of the chance to realize their full mental potential. By downplaying the need for more enhancements to campus food, Campus Dining is endangering students' mental and physical health. And until the state of campus food improves, Campus Dining will only serve as a menace to the health of Cal Poly students.

Lauren Goette is a Psychology major.

Works Cited

Brody, Simeon. "Can a Better Diet Really Help Improve Mental Health?" *Community Care U.K.* Reed Business Information Ltd, 26 Jan. 2006. EBSCO Host. 23 Feb. 2014.

Condon, Garret. "No Secrets to Staying Healthy; Fitness, Nutrition, Rest Are Best Immune-System Boost: [Statewide Edition]." *Hartford Courant.* n.p., 22 Jan. 2004. Web. 3 Mar. 2014.

"Fine (Campus) Dining: Amid Dining Adaptations, Students Continue to Question Campus Food Practices." *Mustang News.* Cal Poly San Luis Obispo, 11 April 2011. Web. 18 Feb. 2014.

Kochakian, Charles. "Nutrition is Important Factor in Education Gap?" 27 March 2012. Proquest. 23 Feb. 2014.

Kolodinsky, Jane. "The Use of Nutritional Labels by College Students in a Food-Court Setting." *Journal of American College Health* (2008): 297–302.

McMinn, Sean. "Facebook Photo Claims to Show Way-too-Rare Campus Dining Meat." *Mustang News.* Cal Poly San Luis Obispo, 14 Jan. 2014. Web. 02 Mar. 2014.

CONSIDER THIS

- Goette repeats the phrase, "we must demand a change," in her introductory paragraph. Does employing such a rhetorical strategy grab your attention as a reader? How does it heighten the tone of the essay from the onset?

- The writer shares her personal experiences early in her argument. Does this choice build her ethos? In what other ways does the writer's personal experience affect her argument? Does her choice to hone in on the experience of a vegan student limit her argument in any way?

- This essay was written before Student Affairs began directing Campus Dining (see the link to the article in the "Look Here" section for more information about that change). Given the recent transition and Vice President Keith Humphrey's commitment to student health, how might the writer update her argument?

In Vitro Meat: Unnatural or Life Saving?

Joseph Coplon

Reflective Memo: *I feel that one of the most difficult parts of writing an essay is choosing a topic. An interesting topic leads to thought-provoking questions that provide fertile ground for writing a research-focused essay. I believe the topic of in vitro meat was perfect for the kind of essay I wanted to write. It's a technology that is still in its early stages of development, but it is not so far off that it seems irrelevant to our modern world. There are plenty of arguments for and against the use of in vitro meat, ranging from environmental issues to questions about ethics. I enjoyed researching the different views on in vitro meat.*

Every year, billions of animals endure terrible suffering and are eventually slaughtered for the purpose of human consumption. The inhumane practices behind producing and distributing the meat of these animals is responsible for enormous amounts of pollution, as well as the waste of land, water, and energy. However, a potential solution exists in the form of in vitro meat, or meat grown synthetically using cells extracted from live animals. This method would dramatically reduce the amount of livestock needed to sustain humanity's demand, while also reducing the strain on the environment caused by the meat industry. Also called cultured meat, in vitro meat is still a developing technology; the question is whether it will provide a viable solution to the ethical and economic problems of conventional meat production.

Beginning in the 1990s, researchers began cultivating stem cells for projects like in vitro meat. William Van Eelen, a World War II survivor, pursued the subject, motivated by his experience with hunger and animal cruelty in a Japanese P.O.W. camp. With the desire to reduce animal suffering and provide a sustainable method for producing meat, he made a breakthrough in 1999 when he received U.S. and international patents for the "Industrial Production of Meat Using Cell Culture Methods" (Schneider 997). Following in Van Eelen's footsteps, the NSR/Touro Applied BioScience Research Consortium produced the first edible sample of cultured meat in 2002, taking the form of fish fillets grown from goldfish cells. Around the same time, NASA began experiments in producing in vitro meat from turkey cells, as in vitro meat could be especially useful in long term space travel. Since then, other laboratories have produced cultured meat from animals like frogs and pigs (Siegelbaum). On August 5, 2013, a Dutch team created the first in vitro burger patty made from cow cells. The burger was then prepared by an expert cook and tasted by food critics and researchers at an event in London. The conclusion of these professionals was that the in vitro beef was extraordinarily close in taste to "real" meat, and was far more authentic than

a soy copy (Zaraska). Despite the steady development of in vitro meat, it is not without adversaries.

Some vegetarians and animal rights activists strongly oppose in vitro meat. One of their key arguments is that in vitro meat does not eliminate animal suffering, as it still requires the cells of donor animals. Current examples of cultured meat require the slaughter of these donor animals, and since DNA of these animals deteriorates when replicated, large-scale production of in vitro meat would require the killing of additional animals. However, in vitro meat is still far more efficient than conventional slaughtering, with estimates placing the amount of meat grown from the stem cells of a donor cow to be 440,000 times the amount gained by processing the meat on a single cow. As production becomes more efficient, fewer and fewer donor animals will be required to feed the world population (Zaraska). Opponents also argue that in vitro meat only addresses the production of meat and thus would have little effect on the cruelty involved

LOOK HERE

In 2008, People for the Ethical Treatment of Animals (PETA) launched a contest to award $1 million to the laboratory that successfully created in vitro chicken. Read an update on the contest here:

http://www.peta.org/features/vitro-meat-contest/

with production of other animal products, such as dairy. The degree of opposition from these protesters varies, with some, like blogger Cheryl Abbate, believing that "experimenting with in vitro meat is a waste of money, energy, time, and resources," because it does not correct every problem related to animal cruelty. This attitude is an example of the perfect solution fallacy and ignores the real goal of in vitro meat research: reducing the number of animals that must be slaughtered while also eliminating the environmental strain of conventional meat production.

Another argument against in vitro meat is that there is no guarantee that it will reduce the demand for conventional meat. Currently, practical production of cultured meats relies upon scaffold-based techniques, which allow for the creation of processed meats like ground beef and hamburgers. Relatively structured meats like steaks are more difficult and expensive to recreate. For many consumers, the label of factory grown meat could create a negative emotional response, and many may object to the replacement of "real" meat with cultured meat. Just as many consumers prefer to eat organic food over genetically modified food, many might wish to eat only "real" meat. However, if the London test of an in vitro hamburger is any indication, cultured meat will be a much closer replica of conventional meat than any previous products. The knowledge that their support

would reduce animal suffering and relieve a strain on the environment may also encourage consumers to convert to cultured meat products.

Finally, opponents of in vitro meat argue that it is prohibitively expensive. The previously mentioned burger tested in London was estimated to have a price tag of over $330,000 (Zaraska). This number is intimidating, but it is worth noting that in vitro meat is still developing rapidly. The real costs of cultured meat are largely unknown. A 2008 study estimated the cost of manufacturing for in vitro meat to be over $5,000 per ton, which is roughly equivalent to the market price of beef in 2008 (Datar 20). A different study put the cost at $5 million per kilogram, which is several orders of magnitude higher (Edelman et al. 671). At either price point, researchers like the Dutch team behind the in vitro burger expect the price to scale down to mass-market prices as the technology grows to industrial levels over the next ten years. It is entirely possible for in vitro versions of ground beef to be economically competitive with existing meat products, so long as a cost effective method is established and aided with government subsidization like that provided to other agricultural businesses (Datar 20). Structured meats may be a little further off, as the technology is far more complex, but the acceptance of scaffold-based cultured meat would provide a strong stepping-stone for research towards this secondary goal.

LOOK HERE

A group of entrepreneurs in Amsterdam started an indiegogo.com campaign to raise money to fund their In Vitro Meat Cookbook. Check out their pitch here:

https://www.indiegogo.com/projects/the-in-vitro-meat-cookbook

Despite the need for further advancements in technology, in vitro meat has many selling points. In particular, one of the greatest advantages of in vitro meat is its potential for beneficially impacting the environment. Studies by researchers Hannah Tuomisto and M. Joost Teixeira de Mattos show that a conversion from conventional meat to cultured meat would reduce energy use by 7–45%, with only poultry having a lower energy use through traditional methods (6120). This effect results from the reduced requirements of maintaining livestock, supplying all the food and water required to support these livestock, using fertilizer and other chemicals, and eliminating the need to transport large amounts of meat across the world. In general, producing in vitro meat is far more efficient than conventional meat, as fewer animals are required, and meat needs to be grown for a period of weeks rather months or years (Edelman et al. 672). Reducing the need for large herds of methane gas producing livestock would contribute to a 78–96% reduction in greenhouse gas emissions and would also lower land use by approximately

99% (Tuomisto and Teixeira de Mattos 6120). As methods of in vitro production advance, energy use could be further reduced. Overall, in vitro meat is far more sustainable and environmentally friendly than conventional meat production.

The reduced volume of inputs required to produce in vitro meat is not only environmentally friendly but also carries a number of benefits for consumers. The growing phenomenon of 3D printing demonstrates the potential for household goods to be made locally, eliminating the costs of shipping such items from factories in other countries. Similarly, production of in vitro meat could be localized and tailored to the desires of buyers, without having to worry about the costs of maintaining large stocks of animals and shipping meat across the world. Restaurants could have in vitro meat machines in their kitchens, allowing far more freedom in the variety of meats on their menus. Customers could order exotic meats to be grown at a local supermarket. Getting such rare meats through in vitro methods would make them more available while reducing the number of endangered species driven close to extinction by the global trade for their flesh (Edelman et al. 672). The same machines could be used in skyscrapers or underground, allowing for more real estate to be used by other industries. Such machines could also be used in space ships to facilitate travel to other planets or solar systems (Siegelbaum).

In vitro meat also has the potential to improve human health. Conventional meat leads to the spread of disease, especially bacterial infections. Many meat farms use the same antibiotics on animals that are used for humans, and as a result antibiotic-resistant strains of bacteria are created that are especially harmful for humans. As this practice continues, more and more bacteria will become immune to common antibiotics. In vitro meat would be far more hygienic, eliminating harmful bacteria while also removing the need for hormones and antibiotics used to treat normal meat. Less livestock also means fewer animals kept in close quarters, making for a reduction in infectious diseases that affect both animals and humans, such as swine flu (Billings).

Cultured meat could also be hand tailored to eliminate the harmful effects of a diet dependent on conventional meat. For example, most meats have a high ratio of saturated fatty acids to poly-unsaturated fats. The former of the two is a primary cause of cardiovascular disease, while the second has beneficial effects on blood cholesterol. With in vitro meat, the amount of saturated fat could be reduced, and the amount of poly-unsaturated fat increased to compensate (Edelman et al. 671). At the same time, producers could add other health nutrients, such as Omega-3s (Billings).

In vitro meat is not a perfect solution to the inhumane treatment of animals, and it still has a ways to go before it is economically viable and acceptable by the majority of consumers. However, as human demand for meat continues to rise, it is important to find sustainable methods of supporting animals and the environment. If in vitro becomes the go-to method for meat production, it would reduce the number of suffering animals, give several health benefits to consumers, and alleviate a huge burden on the environment.

Joseph Coplon is an Electrical Engineering major.

Works Cited

Abbate, Cheryl. "6 Reasons Why You Should Not Support in vitro Meat!" *Thoughts From a Vegan-Feminist-Philosopher-Military Officer.* 13 Aug. 2013. Web. 13 Nov. 2013.

Billings, Lee. "Jason Matheny on the World's Addiction to Meat and How to Grow Ground Beef in a Test Tube." *Seed Magazine.* Seed Media Group, 31 Aug. 2009. Web. 13 Nov. 2013.

Datar, Betti. "Possibilities for an in vitro Meat Production System." *Innovative Food Science and Emerging Technologies* 11 (2010): 13–22. Web. 13 Nov. 2013.

Edelman, P. D., Douglas McFarland, V. A. Mironov, and J. G. Matheny. "Commentary: in vitro-Cultured Meat Production." *Tissue Engineering* 11.5–6 (2005): 659–662. Web. 9 Oct. 2013.

Schneider, Zachary. "in vitro Meat: Space Travel, Cannibalism, and Federal Regulation." *Houston Law Review* 50.991 (2013): 992–1024. Web. 13 Nov. 2013.

Siegelbaum, D.J. "In Search of a Test-Tube Hamburger." *Time.* Time Inc., 23 Apr. 2008. Web. 13 Nov. 2013.

Tuomisto, Hanna L., and M. Joost Teixeira de Mattos. "Environmental Impacts of Cultured Meat Production." *Environmental Science & Technology* 45.14 (2011): 6117–6123. Web. 9 Oct. 2013.

Zaraska, Marta. "Lab-Grown Beef Taste Test: 'Almost' Like a Burger." *Washington Post.* Washington Post Newsweek Interactive, 5 Aug. 2013. Web. 13 Nov. 2013.

Public Rhetoric

CONSIDER THIS

- Coplon develops his argument by addressing the opposition from the outset. This organizational technique has its pros and cons. Does such a choice work given the topic of his essay? Why or why not? What other options do writers have when structuring their arguments?

- The writer chooses not to include in his essay the fact that PETA supports the production of in vitro meat. Discuss with your classmates how incorporating that fact might help or hinder his argument.

- Argumentative essays tend to be more convincing when writers provide background information on their sources when integrating research because it establishes the sources' credibility. Identify moments in this essay when doing so would have enhanced the evidence.

- Given what you have learned about in vitro meat from this essay, rhetorically analyze the indiegogo.com cookbook funding campaign provided in the "Look Here" section.

How Many More?

Allison Aggarwal

Reflective Memo: *Writing this essay meant a lot to me because I felt like I was giving a voice to those who are typically overlooked by society. Not only is this an important issue that deserves more exposure, but also it is especially significant to me because I could have easily been a statistic on a page in someone else's essay. It is time that equal treatment becomes a priority in all our lives and that we create a truly tolerant environment for all kinds of people to feel comfortable with who they are. This is my attempt to begin that transition by raising awareness about the treatment of the LGBT community.*

I love you mom and dad.because even though you did not undertand maybe you loved me and said I was fine and you would help me.but at school it was like being in hell. Iwas burning in hell eery day. I dould not tell you edeverythin thatwas happening. I did not want you to worryaboyut me. I coulnd not do that do you. I hope that youwill forgive me.plese forgive me…Don't be sad. You wont have a faggot son anymore. So you will be happy. No more burden for you. Tell everyone I got sick or something it doesn't matter I just cant go on one day more I cannot fucking go on. (qtd. in Caruso)

This is an excerpt of a letter written by a 16-year-old student named Steven who was severely bullied for being gay. After Steven wrote this, he attempted suicide by overdosing on medication. Although his attempt was unsuccessful, many other gay students are never given a second chance on life.

From news articles to campaigns to court hearings, cases like these are becoming all too familiar nowadays. Teenagers are singled out and ridiculed for their sexual orientation, pushing them to take drastic measures simply to stop the unbearable torment. But with the recent increase in youth "coming out of the closet" and identifying as lesbian, gay, bisexual, or transgendered (LGBT), why hasn't the perpetuating cycle of bullying and suicide ceased among this community? This allows me to conclude that despite their stronger presence today, the never-ending discriminatory treatment against LGBT youth, sustained by society's lack of understanding, leads them to the devastating—but all too common—end result of suicide. So although incorporating appropriate programs that teach inclusivity in schools is vital to improving the overall treatment of this LGBT population, we as individuals must do

> **LOOK HERE**
>
> Learn more about how you can support LGBT equal rights at the Human Rights Campaign website:
>
> **http://www.hrc.org**

our part to create a tolerant social environment by truly living out the message of equality.

With all the recent exposure in the news regarding same sex rights, it seems as if the presence of the LGBT community is increasing in our current society, especially on the college level. In the article, "Suicide Prevention for LGBT Students," from the journal *New Directions for Student Services*, the authors reference a 2010 survey by the American College Health Association that states, "7.2 percent of U.S. college students identify themselves as lesbian, gay, or bisexual" with a few transgendered students on each campus (Johnson et al. 55). To put this into perspective, last year there were 17,680 undergraduate students attending Cal Poly. Of those 17 thousand students, about 12% of those students were of Asian nationality ("Cal Poly"). That means the estimated number of LGBT students at Cal Poly is more than half the Asian population on campus. Now imagine this in the context of all colleges in the United States—that's definitely a significant amount. However, even with this substantial number of students in the LGBT college community, the treatment of these individuals is not improving.

It is safe to say that at one point in most of our lives we have seen or been involved in some form of bullying, whether it was spreading rumors, being excluded, name calling, online harassment, etc. However, these rates tend to be disturbingly high for those in the LGBT youth community and make LGBT youth more prone to mental health conditions. In fact, GLSEN, the Gay, Lesbian, and Straight Education Network, conducted a survey in 2011 that reported "71.3% of students hear homophobic remarks like "dyke" or "faggot"

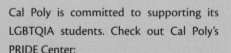

LOOK HERE

Cal Poly is committed to supporting its LGBTQIA students. Check out Cal Poly's PRIDE Center:

http://studentlife.calpoly.edu/pride/

frequently used at school, 81.9% of LGBT sudents are verbally harassed (e.g., called names or threatened), 38.3% were physically harassed (e.g., pushed or shoved), 18.3% were physically assaulted (e.g., punched, kicked, injured with a weapon), and 55.2% experienced electronic harassment, or cyberbullying (via text messages or postings on Facebook)" all because of their sexual orientation (5). The actions and words of their peers, whether intentionally malicious or just purely ignorant, can cause more than just emotional and physical pain for LGBT youth. The survey concluded that students who encountered higher victimization rates based on their sexual orientation experienced much higher levels of depression—about 68% compared to 38% of low victimization students (11). It is these

increased levels of harassment that cause LGBT students to become more susceptible to mental health concerns like depression, which is directly associated with suicidal tendencies. The gross mistreatment that youth in the LGBT community consistently endure often gives them fewer reasons to continue living than their heterosexual peers who face less emotional adversity (Johnson et al. 56). The mental well being of a person can come down to simply the way we choose to treat them. So choosing to deny LGBT individuals fair treatment may directly influence their conclusion that life is no longer worth living.

Constant verbal and physical abuse from peers causes many LGBT students to search for an escape from their troubled reality. Unfortunately, the endless amount of bullying can become so unbearable that these individuals decide there is only one way to solve all their problems—take their own life. The Suicide Prevention Resource Center states that, due to the fact that sexual orientation isn't listed as a cause of death in suicide cases, it's hard to tell just how many of them have been brought upon by LGBT youth harassment. So instead, we can look at the number of LGBT youth who have attempted suicide to get a more accurate estimation of just how common suicide is among this community. As it turns out, LGBT youth are up to seven times more likely than non-LGBT youth to have attempted suicide, making it the leading cause of death in the LGBT community as compared to it being the third leading cause for the general youth population ("Suicide risk" 13). The fact that the likelihood of committing suicide differs between two very similar populations, simply separated by sexual orientation, suggests that there is in fact a problem in the treatment of LGBT youth. The harsh criticism from their peers and society for having a "different" sexual preference coerces LGBT students into seeking an alternative place where they can truly be themselves without prejudice. In thinking a place like this will never exist, they come to the ultimate decision that they must look for it beyond the realm of living.

Although there are many gay suicide victims, there is one specific case in particular that sparked national awareness of this issue. Tyler Clementi was a freshman at Rutgers University in New Jersey. One month into the school year, Clementi and his roommate, Dharun Ravi, encountered serious privacy issues because Ravi was setting up his own webcam to secretly watch Clementi's intimate moments with another male student. One night, Ravi used his laptop webcam to record Clementi and a male student sharing a romantic moment. Ravi decided to stream that footage to his iChat and tweeted it out to many of the Rutgers students to go watch. Not only did this out Clementi as being gay, but it also put his most personal moments on display. The next day, on September 22, 2010, Clementi jumped off the George Washington Bridge into the Hudson River.

After an extensive trial, Ravi was convicted of invasion of privacy, bias intimidation, witness tampering, and hindering arrest due to his attempt to cover up his crime (Parker). As Judge Glenn Berman read the young man's sentence—30 days in jail, 300 hours of community service, 3 years probation, and required attendance to counseling programs for cyber-bullying—he explained to the court, "I do not believe [Ravi] hated Tyler Clementi. He had no reason to, but I do believe he acted out of colossal insensitivity" (Koenigs, Smith, and Ng). Ignorance. Ravi was unaware of how detrimental his actions were going to be on Tyler Clementi's life. Whether this is true or not, his insensitivity could have been prevented by more exposure to the LGBT community. So although this case brought issues of privacy to the public eye, it redefined the severity of bullying and proved the consequences extreme ignorance can have on LGBT students.

What astonishes me most about this cycle of LGBT youth bullying and suicide is that it could be stopped in its tracks by proper education regarding equal treatment for all people. In GLSEN's survey of school climate, they state, "Students in schools with an inclusive curriculum heard fewer

LOOK HERE

Check out the Think B4 You Speak Campaign:

http://www.thinkb4youspeak.com

homophobic remarks, including negative use of the word "gay," the phrase "no homo," and homophobic epithets (e.g., "fag" or "dyke"), and fewer negative comments about someone's gender expression than those without an inclusive curriculum" (15). By being in an environment where respect is the basic core value behind how students treat one another, ideas like being more accepting of diversity would become a reality through daily interactions. Education is always the best combatant to ignorance, and the ignorance we face today targets people that are unknown or different from us—like the LGBT community. We must continue to create more environments, especially in schools, where all students, regardless of their sexual orientation, feel safe and equal. In doing this, we will start to drastically reduce the amount of harassment LGBT students experience and hopefully prevent more tragic suicides from occurring.

The fact is that although the presence of the LGBT youth community is growing substantially, their all-too-frequent encounters with severe bullying pushes these individuals to extremes to make it stop. They seek an escape from the harsh reality that awaits them everyday at school as well as in the general community. I am not naïve to think everyone will be accepting of differing lifestyles, but we need to realize that we are not entitled to act upon our personal discontent of the sexuality of others. We must learn to foster an environment where LGBT youth can breathe knowing their sexual orientation will not define

the way they are treated. We need to take matters into our own hands to bring about a time where our differing characteristics do not define our social standing. Currently, LGBT students are at a disadvantage because everything around us caters to a hetero-normative society. We ask girls if they have a boyfriend; we ask guys if they are going to hit on the super hot girl at the party; we use the word "gay" as a derogatory insult for men who act feminine. We must educate ourselves on the importance of fair treatment of all people, regardless of sexual orientation. Eric James Borges, a 19-year-old victim of gay bullying, chose these as his last words before taking his own life: "My pain is not caused because I am gay. My pain is caused by how I was treated because I am gay" ("Eric James"). So how many more of these stories do we need to read before it is time to make change? How many more?

Allison Aggarwal is a Sociology major.

Works Cited

"Cal Poly San Luis Obispo: Student Profile." *CSU Mentor*. 27 June 2013. Web. 11 Feb. 2014.

Caruso, Kevin. "Suicide Note of a Gay Teen." *Suicide.org*. n.p., n.d. Web. 11 Feb. 2014.

"Eric James Borges' Suicide Note, Memorial Service Sheds New Insight into Bullied Gay Teen's Life." *Huffington Post*. 01 Jan. 2012. Web. 11 Feb. 2014.

Gay, Lesbian and Straight Education Network (GLSEN). "The 2011 National School Climate Survey: Key Findings on the Experiences of Lesbian, Gay, Bisexual and Transgender Youth in our Nation's Schools. Executive Summary." *Gay, Lesbian And Straight Education Network (GLSEN)*. 2012. *ERIC*. Web. 11 Feb. 2014.

Johnson, Bradley R., Symphony Oxendine, Deborah J. Taub, and Jason Robertson. "Suicide Prevention for LGBT Students." *New Directions for Student Services*. n. 141: pg. 55–69. 2013. *Wiley Online Library*. Web. 11 Feb. 2014.

Koenigs, Michael, Candance Smith, and Christina Ng. "Rutgers Trial: Dharun Ravi Sentenced to 30 Days in Jail." *ABC News*. 21 May 2012. Web. 04 Mar. 2014.

Parker, Ian. "The Story of a Suicide." *New Yorker*. 2012. *EBSCOhost*. Web. 11 Feb. 2014. "Suicide risk and prevention for lesbian, gay, bisexual, and transgender youth." *Suicide Prevention Resource Center*. 2008. Education Development Center, Inc. Web. 11 Feb. 2014.

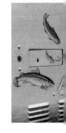

CONSIDER THIS

- Aggarwal begins her essay with an excerpt from a gay teen's suicide note. What kind of tone does the writer set by doing so? Does the excerpt from the note draw you into the topic in a particular way?

- Halfway through the essay and again in the conclusion, the writer uses the term "we," directly calling herself and her readers into action. How did you as a reader experience those moments? Was such a choice effective in encouraging you to consider the treatment of LGBT peers?

- Like the beginning, the writer concludes the essay with the voice of another LGBT youth's suicide note. How does the statement by Eric James Borges affect your stance on this topic after engaging in the essay?

- Aggarwal incorporates statistics to help make her case. Locate the stats she uses and discuss with your classmates how such evidence helps her argument. Consider other types of evidence the writer might have incorporated to enhance her argument.

Human Trafficking

Ikhlaus Ahmed

Reflective Memo: *Writing this essay was a wonderful experience. I became more informed about the issue. The main challenges I faced were page constraints and the amount of time given. I could have easily written 1–2 pages more on the issue. My favorite part of the essay was including the perspective of two trafficked victims because doing so gives the audience a sense of what human trafficking is actually like. Overall it was a fantastic experience writing this essay, and it helped me build on my research skills.*

No one knows what has become of you. You are snatched away from your family, shoved into a dark box feeling lost with hopelessness. You are shackled in chains, dehumanized, and prepared to become property. One moment you are an innocent child and in an instant you are tossed into a life of slavery, doomed with endless labor. The life of a child is meant to be filled with joy and happiness, not filled with hurt and misery. Sadly, this horror is the reality that is forced upon thousands of children every year through the terrors of human trafficking. Despite human trafficking being recognized globally, there is no international solution or effective strategies to have it reach its demise. Nations should work together and form a committee to combat human trafficking through actively searching for human traffickers.

Human trafficking is a drastic and modern form of slavery. Two main types of human trafficking include labor trafficking and sex trafficking. Labor trafficking is defined as forcing one to work for little to no pay. This form of trafficking generally requires the victims to perform arduous labor, and they are often treated as slaves—beaten and punished. Sex trafficking occurs through commercial sex trade, involving an individual (male or female) forced into sex acts. Victims of sex trafficking are abused and raped without mercy. A common misconception about human trafficking is that it usually takes place in developing countries, which is not necessarily the case. Human trafficking is encountered throughout the world including the United States and Europe. It occurs on a transnational level, meaning victims are often kidnapped in one country and sold in another—making their rescue rate extremely low. The commonality that all victims of human trafficking share is that they are generally promised a better life, receive both physical and mental abuse, and have little chance of escape.

Human trafficking exists because like any other criminal business it has a demand. Human trafficking is a "market-driven criminal industry that is based on the principles of supply and demand" ("Human Trafficking"). The demand comes from the need for cheap labor or desire for commercial sex acts. Human

traffickers manipulate and abuse people simply for money and cheap labor. Human trafficking is thriving because it is both "low risk" and immensely high in profits. It is low risk mainly due to the fact that there is not much awareness of the issue. If the general public were aware that human trafficking is an issue in today's society the government would have a solid plan in action to combat it. Human labor and sex trafficking is high in profits because "when individuals are willing to buy commercial sex, they create a market and make it profitable for traffickers to sexually exploit children and adults. When consumers are willing to buy goods and services from industries that rely on forced labor, they create a profit incentive for labor traffickers to maximize revenue with minimal production costs" ("Human Trafficking"). This shows that individuals are willing to pay for coerced labor that allows for exploitation and abuse. However, this is primarily because a majority of the general public is not aware that a portion of the labor that produces their goods and services basically comes from human slaves. Thus, human trafficking occurs because not only is it cheap labor, but also because it allows for easy profits. The awareness of this issue must increase in order to begin combating human trafficking.

The life of a trafficked victim is filled with deep sorrow. For example, Nadia, a needy women from Moldova, was targeted and taken across Europe after being offered "a restaurant job in Italy" ("Italy and Moldova"). Nadia accepted the offer primarily because she was in desperate need of money. She was completely unaware of the horrors that lay ahead and hoped for a better life. Nadia was raped "countless times"—at one point she was forced to have sex with "twenty-five individuals" in one day; her sex traffickers were ruthless and "would occasionally throw her a punch or put a gun to her head" to remind her that she was property ("Italy and Moldova"). The treatment that Nadia received was inhumane and degrading. She is only one victim out of thousands that has faced the same atrocity. An example of human trafficking within the United States was of a victim by the name of Dai, a Korean American Citizen. Her story falsifies the notion that human trafficking does not affect U.S citizens, thus proving that human trafficking can exist in a nation of laws such as the United States. Dai's experience with human trafficking involved being raped, locked in a closet as a form of punishment, begging for her life, and witnessing the beatings, rapes and murders of other women ("A Survivor's Story"). Her experiences are just as terrible as Nadia's, if not worse. Luckily, both of them were able to escape and were not trafficked for more than 6 months. There are stories of people's lives that are far worse than Nadia's and Dai's. Most of them have common endings—the victims escape. None of them were rescued by the police or authorities.

Currently, the only real measures that are being taken against human trafficking are increasing the awareness of the issue, working towards prevention, and providing counseling and rehabilitation resources for victims. Human trafficking is a global issue, yet the issue is mainly combated by organizations not funded by the government. Organizations that currently combat human trafficking include Polaris Project, Unseen, Not for Sale Campaign, and the Council of Europe. Each organization basically takes the same measures to combat human trafficking, but they operate in different countries. Polaris Project mainly operates in the United States, Not for Sale Campaign operates in Japan, Australia, and the U.S., and Unseen primarily functions in the United Kingdom. They all aim to increase the "prevention" of trafficking and provide "survivor's support" ("Aims & Objectives"). To most of the organizations, prevention is raising awareness of the issue and equipping people with the knowledge to recognize and spot signs of human trafficking. Clearly, these organizations are making an effort to prevent trafficking. Survivor's support for victims of human trafficking is usually counseling, rehabilitation services, and shelters. For example, Unseen opened up a safe house for women two years ago and has since seen over "60 women" ("It Might Look"). A lot of these organizations really do their best to assist victims of human trafficking. They are doing their part in trying to serve the victims of human trafficking, but is it enough? In 2012, there were about "2,225 potential cases of human trafficking recorded in the UK" and the actual numbers are "recognised as much higher" ("It Might Look"). Those statistics are only for the United Kingdom. Through viewing those numbers, one could easily come to the conclusion that the current solution is not satisfactory. It should not be simply a bunch of organizations taking actions against human trafficking; governments should be involved.

LOOK HERE

In June 2014, the FBI rescued 168 young people from sex trafficking in the U.S. Read about it here:

http://thinkprogress.org/justice/2014/06/24/3452385/sex-trafficking/

LOOK HERE

See how you can engage your community in the fight against human trafficking:

http://www.polarisproject.org/resources/outreach-and-awareness-materials/student-toolkit

To combat human trafficking properly, governments should work together internationally; however, they must start at the community level. There first needs to be awareness within our communities that human trafficking "is considered to be one of the fastest growing criminal industries in the world" and that it generates "billions of dollars in profits by victimizing millions of people around the world" ("Human Trafficking"). They need to realize that human trafficking takes place within the United States and other first world countries, not just the developing world. Through making communities aware of the horrors of human trafficking, individuals would be more likely to want to take action against it and push for legislation that takes more serious courses of action against human trafficking. Only after governments realize this is a real issue through its citizens will they begin to take a more serious course of action.

As well, since human trafficking occurs on a transnational level, governments should work together internationally to form a task force that actively searches for human traffickers and prosecutes them. The task force should seek out traffickers through undercover work, accounts from recently escaped victims, and studies of forms of communication such as emails, texting, and phone calls. The issue needs to be treated as a form of terrorism and all governments should seek out human traffickers just as they would do with terrorists. Human traffickers should be treated as terrorists because rather than killing the victims, they make the victims wish they were dead, which is just as evil, if not worse. Overall, to combat human trafficking properly, awareness needs to be raised within communities and the government should hunt out human traffickers as they would with terrorists.

However, some people may believe that the current measures are enough to combat human trafficking. In January and early February 2014, "a multistate operation led to the arrests of 359 men soliciting sex and 14 others who were arrested on sex trafficking charges" (Norfleet). There currently are measures that are being taken to search for and prosecute traffickers. This is only one story of the immense amount of human trafficking arrests lately. Regardless, the main pattern that occurs with a majority of the arrests is that they revolve around immense sporting events within the United States. The arrests in the article above revolve around Super Bowl Sunday. Clearly, the United States is currently doing an incredible job at prosecuting sex traffickers. However, we are mainly capturing sex traffickers. What about the labor traffickers? According to Peter Rocco from the Human Trafficking Center:

> When the Olympic Games open today in Sochi, Russia, television viewers will no doubt be treated to views of brand new stadiums and other displays of Vladimir Putin's largesse. Unfortunately, NBC's commentators will likely not point out that the glittering infrastructure was built by the forced labor of migrants from places such as Kyrgyzstan, Serbia and Ukraine. Since Russia was awarded the Games in 2007, tens of thousands of workers have cycled through hundreds of projects that have transformed the Sochi area.

Labor trafficking is recognized as a common form of human trafficking, yet there are rarely any articles about people getting prosecuted for labor trafficking. One may conclude from the amount of articles about sex trafficking when compared to the amount on labor trafficking that labor trafficking is not a real issue. Clearly, the current measures that are in place against human trafficking are inadequate.

Human trafficking is one of the most urgent issues in the world today, constantly affecting millions of lives across the globe. When people usually hear "affecting millions of lives," they tend to think of developing countries. What about the stories of Nadia and Dai? Their experiences were in first world countries—Dai's experience was even within the U.S. Their stories were just as dreadful as, if not worse than, the lives of people affected by the war on terror. What if human trafficking was combated with the equivalent amount of effort that the nations use to seek out terrorists? The current measures being taken against human trafficking are clearly substandard because they involve hoping for prevention and increasing awareness. Countries should be dedicating more money and resources to this serious issue, but as individuals we also should do our best to raise awareness of the issue through perhaps writing a letter to our senators or inviting speakers to our campuses to talk about human trafficking. The issue of human trafficking is one that everyone should be aware of; with enough people aware of the issue and willing to take action, maybe one day human trafficking will be fought with the same intensity that is given towards terrorists.

Ikhlaus Ahmed is a History major.

Works Cited

"Aims & Objectives." *Unseen UK*. Unseen, n.d. Web. 03 Mar. 2014.

"Human Trafficking." *Polaris Project*. Polaris Project, n.d. Web. 03 Mar. 2014.

"Italy and Moldova—Nadia's Story." *Not For Sale Campaign*. Not For Sale Campaign, n.d. Web. 03 Mar. 2014.

"It might look different, but slavery is very much alive." *The Post*. 17 Jan. 2014. Proquest. Web. 03 Mar. 2014.

Norfleet, N. "1 arrest here in sex-traffic sting." *Star Tribune*. 08 Feb. 2014. Proquest. Web. 03 Mar. 2014.

Rocco, Peter. "Forced Labor at the Sochi Games." *Human Trafficking Center*. Human Trafficking Center, n.d. Web. 03 Mar. 2014.

"A Survivor's Story." *Stophumantraffickingny.wordpress.com*. New York State Anti-Trafficking Coalition, n.d. Web. 03 Mar. 2014.

CONSIDER THIS

- Addressing the reader directly through second person can be a risky stylistic choice because it may alienate the audience; however, this writer chooses to address the reader in his introduction and conclusion. Was this a rewarding stylistic risk? How would the essay change had the writer relied solely on third-person throughout?

- Ahmed offers his readers background information and context surrounding his focus. Why was this necessary? How might the readers' understanding of the topic change had the author not included this information?

- Audiences often mistrust arguments that rely heavily on pathos. How does this author employ pathos? Does he balance the appeal effectively with ethos and logos?

To What Extent?

Carson Dangberg

Where must we draw the line? When has it gone too far? Is it fair or legal for them to take our rights? These concerns over gun control have sparked a worldwide debate. With over 140 countries signing the United Nations Small Arms Treaty, including the United States, pro-gun advocates—including the National Rifle Association (NRA)—have heavily criticized the President saying that this will ultimately lead to the disarming of all American citizens. Hugely overestimating the policies placed by the treaty, these advocates are striking fear into the hearts of every day gun owners. The true issues don't lie in pages of complex government treaties, however; they start with the vicious crimes radiating out of the American public. Finding a way to save civilian lives from violent gun crimes is what needs to be at the top of the priority list. As a gun owner, ethical hunter, and concerned citizen, I am not only aware of the consequences the overuse of gun control produces, but I am also fearful that many guns will get into the hands of the wrong people.

Automatic and semi-automatic assault weapons, usually resembling military grade weaponry, are extremely lethal and used in many heinous crimes. A scary and reoccurring pattern has been brought up from many federal firearms agencies. Special Agent Robert J. Creighton of the Federal Bureau of Alcohol, Tobacco, and Firearms stated, "There has been a tremendous increase in machine guns" (Hollow). With police officers originally carrying .38-caliber revolvers with a 6 round magazine, they could stand no chance against criminals who possessed automatic machine guns like the MAC 10, having the capability of spewing 850 armor piercing bullets at officers per minute. While originally banned under the 1994 Assault Weapons Ban, this deadly machine of war is on the streets now, being used against police officers. In order to save the lives of police officers and innocent civilians, the ban once placed on these military style weapons must be reinstated.

Not only does the automatic and semi-automatic functions of guns play a role in gun related crimes, but magazine size also plays a huge part in gun violence. What practical use does a gun with 30 rounds of ammunition have in a community? The reality of the situation is that it has little to no practical use outside of the military. Yes, many people love to go out to a field somewhere to shoot their big guns at random objects, but it's really unnecessary. This comes to light with the argument of hunting and whether or not it is a necessity to have oversized magazines. Scott Willoughby of the *Denver Post* argues that in the mandatory hunter safety course all hunters complete, they "advocate one shot, one kill, in the field" (Willoughby). He also references that if a hunter requires

more than seven shots, that person should continue to practice and ultimately stop hunting until their marksmanship improves. Being that hunters are sometimes considered marksmen, they should have the skills to use a limited number of shots. And frankly hitting a deer or an elk with 10 or 15 bullets could definitely ruin the meat. The argument that hunters will be extremely affected by a magazine size reduction law is truly invalid, generalizing that all hunters require a high number of rounds to kill their prey. Hunters are some of the most ethical gun owners even though they have a bad reputation sometimes because they are killing animals when some believe it to be thoroughly inhumane. However, this does not mean that they ruthlessly kill using high numbers of bullets, like individuals do in many gun related crimes.

When it is legal to have large capacity magazines? What could stop someone from using those 15–30 round or more magazines to massacre elementary school kids or movie enthusiasts? A *CNN News* article by Daniel Webster showed that in the Aurora, Colorado shooting,

> **LOOK HERE**
>
> For an interactive graphic on recent gun laws, check out this site:
>
> http://www.nytimes.com/interactive/2013/12/10/us/state-gun-laws-enacted-in-the-year-since-newtown.html

the gunman allegedly used a 100 round drum magazine in his massacre. Without having to reload a single magazine, he was able to shoot, injure and/or kill around 70 moviegoers using an assault rifle (Webster 1). Limiting capacity will limit the numbers of lives lost by decreasing the amount of ammo used at once in those tragic but real events. Personally having shot some of these weapons, I can tell you that having to carry 10 extra magazines and reloading 10 times to have the same number of bullets as the shooter makes a difference. One must eject the magazine, unclip the additional magazine from its carrier, insert it into the gun, and close the action—a process taking an additional 3 to 5 seconds per magazine—in order to reload. This creates enough time for the people caught in the crossfire to either escape the area or take cover, preventing casualties. I can admit that just limiting the size of the magazines will not stop someone who is mentally unstable from committing these types of crimes, but it will significantly reduce the deaths and injuries of innocent civilians. The real way to prevent these events from occurring is by preventing such people from obtaining such weaponry.

The epicenter of the violent acts committed by the use of guns is when guns get into the hands of unethical people. Even with the extensive background checks and legal barriers in order to purchase a gun, criminals still get their hands on these machines of death. This needs to stop. In an article from *US Today*, the

author illustrates an alarming phenomenon where individuals go through the background checks and requirements to buy a gun for someone who legally can't. This act of transferring a gun from a legal owner to an illegal one is called a "Straw Purchase." This way all guns that are legally on the market can end up in the hands of the wrong people: criminals, people with mental illnesses, domestic abusers, and even the drug traffickers that the government is working so hard to fight ("Straw Purchases"). In order to pass the background test, someone must not have any criminal charges—felonies—and must not have been institutionalized for having a mental illness (Cannon). In past cases where one of these people got a hold of a firearm, a background check wasn't required. The background checks limit the number of unstable people having access to firearms.

There isn't a "universal" background check that can access every detail and fact about a person; however, checking for illness or criminal activity will most definitely reduce gun violence in city streets. As required by the Brady Law established by President Clinton in 1993, all persons buying a firearm from a licensed dealer must go through a series of

LOOK HERE

The mass shootings in Isla Vista, near the UCSB campus, in May 2014, sparked further gun control debates. Check out this site for ways you can join the fight against gun deaths in your community:

http://everytown.org

checks. In the twenty years since this series of legislations has been implemented, "the Brady Campaign to Prevent Gun Violence reported that at least 2 million purchases have been blocked—more than 1 million of them involving felons" (Kiefer). Seeing the true effectiveness of this bill should spark the interests of all non-believers. This truly astounding number of blocked purchases has kept the streets safer. Stopping criminals from carrying and purchasing weapons has limited the number of violent crimes committed.

Implementing complete gun control, or the confiscation of all guns from all citizens, will never happen. Bearing arms is a right guaranteed by the Constitution. But the fact that so many criminals can get their hands on the extremely dangerous weapons is astounding. By preventing those people from acquiring guns that should be strictly for the military is one way of limiting gun violence. Being that there are already so many guns illegally in the hands of criminals, stopping the crime altogether is impossible. But limiting how many new guns are put onto the streets and into the hands of violent people will stop the crime rate from growing out of control. Order must be kept and lives must be saved. Limiting the size of magazines, banning assault weapons and stopping the sale of guns to the wrong people will certainly help. The safety of American citizens is what is most

important and by implementing several rules, concerns with individual safety will start to fade away.

Carson Dangberg is a Biological Sciences major.

Works Cited

Cannon, Angie. "Guns and the Mentally Ill." *US News and World Report* 132.10 (2002): 22. *Academic Search Premier*. Web. 18 Feb. 2014.

Hollow, Laurel. "Often Outgunned, Police Are Bolstering Firepower." *New York Times* [New York] 27 Sept. 1986: n. pag. Print.

Kiefer, Francine. "Gun-control Activists, Resolute, Cite Merits of Background Checks." *The Christian Science Monitor* [Boston] 28 Feb. 2014: n. pag. *ProQuest Newsstand*. Web. 2 Mar. 2014.

"'Straw Purchases' Put Guns in the Wrong Hands: USA Today." *Academic Search Premier*. EBSCO, 08 Mar. 2013. Web. 18 Feb. 2014.

Webster, Daniel W. "Mass Murder and Powerful Firearms." *CNN.com*. Turner Broadcasting System, Inc., 24 July 2012. Web. 4 Mar. 2014.

Willoughby, Scott. "Colorado's Hunters Overlooked in Gun Control Debate." *The Denver Post*. The Denver Post, 13 Mar. 2013. Web. 19 Feb. 2014.

CONSIDER THIS

- At the beginning of the essay, Dangberg admits to being a gun owner. How does such information help or hinder his credibility?

- The writer addresses hunters and the ethics of firing one shot versus multiple shots in the field. As a reader, does his discussion of hunting help you transform your position on gun control? If so, how? And, if not, then how might you have recommended the writer revise that section of the essay?

- Dangberg takes an interesting approach to the topic of gun control in that he maintains a narrow focus on what is generally a very complex topic. What are the components of gun control this writer advocates for? How does his narrow focus strengthen his argument?

Not A Monster

Jessica Hadley

Reflective Memo: *As you can tell from this essay, I care a lot about wolves. The white wolf (540F) inspired my dream to become a wolf biologist. Seeing her, my first wild wolf, is something I'm never going to forget. Even though it has been years since she was killed by another pack in 2007, I hope to aid her descendants in their fights against the government's proposal to delist wolves from the endangered species act in the lower 48 states.*

Staring across the Yellowstone River into the eyes of the very beast I had only ever dreamed of seeing, I realized this was not the monster described in one of my favorite books, Jack London's *White Fang*. Wolves are not monsters. They do not eat humans; they rarely do anything but run away from us. However, as a result of their negative image portrayed by the media, many people in the United States believe that wolves are harmful creatures; they are blind to the glorious advantages this animal brings to America's wilderness.

The vast territory of the wolf once stretched across the United States, and began to diminish after becoming prey to man who hunted them down to the last wolf in 1943. In 1995, the gray wolf was reintroduced to Yellowstone National Park where packs began to flourish, making one

> ### Look Here
>
> Watch this documentary on the reintroduction of wolves into Yosemite:
>
> **http://www.pbs.org/wnet/nature/ episodes/in-the-valley-of-the-wolves/ introduction/212/**

of the most successful comebacks that the Endangered Species Act has ever experienced. But today, after what many thought was the end, man once again hunts the wolf for reasons similar to those that led to the extermination of this animal over 85 years ago. Ranchers and hunters alike have declared war on wolves, believing them to be ruthless killers greatly affecting both elk populations and livestock. However, I believe the wolf has been given a false image described as vicious and dangerous by the media, but they are truly timid animals; they are a key species to their environment by preventing elk from overpopulating and affecting the entire ecosystem as a whole.

For years, ranchers and hunters have invented conflict with wolves, fearing for their livestock, their own families, and even big game supplies. Ranchers have always struggled to live in the presence of wolves because, as predators, they often come as a threat to livestock. "During 2008, wildlife agents confirmed 569 cattle

and sheep deaths from wolves throughout the west" (Chadwick 2). Ranchers are running a business not just a farm. Loss of animals to wolves is more then just upsetting; it's also loss of money. Not only do wolves just hunt the livestock, but they can also affect the animal's health by an increase in stress. In cattle this often results in a lower birth rate meaning even more livestock lost to wolves: "We had 85 pregnant heifers this spring, and 60 aborted" (Chadwick 3). The stress can also cause other problems as well. Cattle often "come off the pasture on average about 100 pounds lighter than before there were wolves in the area" (Kaufman 2). Rancher's work becomes increasingly more frustrating with this growing presence of the wolf. Their first instinct upon seeing a wolf is to shoot. Old stories have led them to automatically protect their animals, land, and family from this predator that once threatened their ancestors' ways of living. It's a sort of "'shoot first, ask questions never' policy" easily seen in Mr. Peterson's case; he did not even pause before shooting the wolf he spotted on his property (Boyce 1; Kaufman 1). People often feel discomfort knowing wolves are now sharing the environment. Some even say "they no longer feel as safe taking their families into the woods" (Chadwick 2). Wolves overall harm a rancher's business and sense of security, but when they are not causing "livestock deprivation" they are also "ravaging game populations" (Tabish 1; Chadwick 2). Many hunters complain "about wolves overrunning the place and wiping out elk and deer" (Chadwick 6). So, to solve this problem, hunters and ranchers have pushed for wolf hunts—which are now underway—and are also allowing for trapping. After Minnesota's first wolf season, "hunters killed 413 wolves. The DNR (Department of Natural Resources) estimates the state's population to be 'stable' at 3,000" (Tabish 2). By keeping wolf populations down, hunters have more supply of game as well as a new species to hunt.

Maybe the reason hunters and ranchers have such a huge problem with the wolf is because they fear it—fear the way this creature could affect their surroundings. But this fear is dangerous. It blinds them to the simple reality: the facts that show this animal is not a ruthless killer. In most cases, wolves prefer their natural prey to rancher's livestock, "I've seen wolves walk right through cattle herds to stalk deer" (Chadwick 4). When wolves do attack livestock, it is not as severe a loss as many believe it to be. "In 2010, according to the USDA, wolves killed 8,100 head of cattle… That's only 3.7 percent of the total of other predators; coyotes…account for 53.1 percent, or 116,700 head of cattle…dogs (21,800 head)…mountain lions, bobcats, and lynx (18,900 head)" (Nosowitz 2). Also, wolves are blamed for killing off big game, but "Northwestern Montana has at least twice as many cougars as wolves and twice as many grizzly bears. Together they kill more adult deer and fawns than wolves do" (Chadwick 6). Killing off the wolves would not solve the issue of lost livestock or big game animals, but killing

off these other predatory animals is not the solution either; this would only cause further problems. But even if all animals were out of the picture they only make up a fraction of livestock deaths, but still wolves continue to be subject to the most criticism. In Oregon "what started to happen was every single dead cow was of course a wolf kill…further investigations were showing…that wasn't the case…In 2010, fewer than a dozen cows and calves were killed by wolves compared to 55,000 lost to disease, weather and other causes" (Peterson 2).

Ranchers have not been left to deal with the wolf on their own. Programs have been established to help them by "offering them money and tools to fend off wolves without killing them" and also to provide compensation for lost animals (Kaufman 1). However, ranchers have been ignorant and unwilling to compromise in most cases. As Mr. Peterson put it, "a lot of my neighbors think I am wet behind the ears to take money from these people" (qtd. in Kaufman 1). But these tactics are working despite their resistance. In Montana, "the amount of livestock killed has shrunk since 2009… A total of 370 claims were filed… there were 175 claims in 2010 and 95 in 2011" (Tabish 2). Even with the lower numbers of livestock deaths, ranchers and hunters have continued to push for hunting.

Wolf hunts are now becoming more common and the number of wolves killed has been rising. The wolf has been pushed to, as U.S. Fish and Wildlife Director Dan Ashe put it, "bare-minimum-survival" (The War on Wolves 1). Killing wolves is unnecessary. They are important to the environment and there is no need for them to be "subject[ed] to so much irrational slaughter" (The War on Wolves 1). In 1949, Aldo Leopold wrote, "We reached the old wolf in time to watch a fierce green fire dying in her eyes… I thought that… fewer wolves meant more deer… no wolves would mean hunters' paradise. But after seeing the green fire die, I sensed that neither the wolf nor the mountain agreed with such a view" (Anderson 3). Killing wolves seems like a great idea to those who see them as frightening, but this creature is no monster. "Cristina Eisenberg is a five-foot-two-inch, hundred-pound answer to the question of how dangerous wolves are to people" (Chadwick 6). Eisenberg has spent four years studying "wolves, elk, and aspen in Glacier Park… among two large wolf packs, one with 20-plus members" (Chadwick 6). She has never been attacked. Daniel MacNulty, a wildlife-ecology professor at Utah State University, explains that "Most people don't realize this, but wolves are wimps" (Berlin 2). In Daniel's "16 years of studying wolves in Yellowstone National Park," he has "never been approached by a wolf or wolf pack" (Berlin 1). However, in the cases found when wolves do attack humans, nearly all the wolves were rabid (Nosowitz 3). But the number of wolf attacks is still incredibly low, none since 1995, and only 20 to 30 in the 20th century with only 3 being fatal (Nosowitz 3). "In that same 100-year period, there were 71 fatal attacks from brown bears…and about 17 people die every year from dog

attacks" (Nosowitz 3). The wolf is not a creature we need to fear; it is less harmful then many other species, such as the coyote, and much more helpful to the environment then many other creatures we let live.

During the years when the wolf was absent from Yellowstone National Park, a discovery was made: the environment was dying without its most powerful predator. In the absence of the wolf, elk and coyotes took over the area. "Elk herds were destroying large tracts of vegetation, and coyotes had reduced second-tier predators" (Kaufman 2). The beaver soon became extinct in Yellowstone because of a lack of aspen and cotton wood trees needed to support a beaver colony. By 1996, Doug Smith, "surveying the huge northern range… turned up just one beaver colony… the lowest tally in decades" (Chadwick 5). But after the reintroduction of the wolf, the vegetation started to make a comeback and by 2009, Smith recorded twelve beaver colonies (Chadwick 5). Beaver colonies are important to the ecosystem, helping provide habitat for species such as "moose, muskrat, mink, waterfowl, wading birds, and an array of other wildlife" (Chadwick 5). In Glacier National Park, aspen trees reveal the damage caused by the removal of wolves from their environment. "Its upper tier consists of towering trees that arose between 1840 and the 1920s, before wolves were eliminated. The bottom row, 15 feet high, is of saplings that shot up after wolves returned. There are no aspens in between. None got past the elks' mouths" (Chadwick 6). The wolf overall helps the elk population by keeping it in control, making them stronger. "Wolves prey on the weak and feeble; by culling the elk herd in this way, the remaining elk tend to be stronger and healthier" (Nosowitz 3). Also, in the absence of the wolves, as a "second-tier predator," foxes began to disappear from the park unable to deal with the growing coyote population. With the reintroduction of the wolf, these "big canines killed nearly half the coyote population," allowing for foxes to make a comeback (Chadwick 5). The benefits that the wolves bring don't stop at the environment. "In Yellowstone alone, tens of thousands come to watch wolves each year, adding an estimated $35 million to the area's economy" (Chadwick 2). Leo Cottenoir responsible for the death of the last wolf in 1943 said, "I still think they ought to have wolves in there. They are a native animal, native to the country and something that has always been there" (qtd. in "The Last Wolf" 1).

Media has convinced the world that wolves are evil killing machines, ruthless when humans cross their paths. This patterns is easily seen in Liam Neeson's movie, *The Grey*, classic books, such as Jack London's *White Fang*, and even children stories, like *Little Red Riding Hood* and *The Three Little Pigs*. The wolves have been "caricatured throughout history as cunning, yellow-eyed monsters" and never the powerful species that contributes so much to the health of its environment (Boyce 1). The problem with a lot of the media is that most of it seems pretty real to the people who don't know much about wolves. However, Jack London's use of the wolf as a man-eater is explained by K.A. Applegate in the introduction to *White Fang*: "London's wolves aren't wolves as wolves are, they're wolves as he wanted them to be, as he needed them to be… London's people are like London's wolves" (London). The wolf has always played the bad guy because it makes a good story, but the wolf also shares similar qualities with humans. Maybe the problem we have with wolves is because they are like us, strong and intelligent, powerfully affecting their surroundings, caring for their packs; they aren't so different from us. But then why are we teaching our children to fear such an important animal? Children learn to fear these animals at such a young age, told they could be eaten just like in *Little Red Riding Hood* and *The Three Little Pigs*. There are few stories in which the wolf is not to be feared. Perhaps if more children grew up seeing wolves in a positive story like scientist Jane Goodall did, fewer would grow up accepting wolves as something to fear. "My love of wolves began when I was a child and read the story of Mowgli, the Jungle Boy who was adopted by Mother Wolf and Father Wolf and raised with their pups," (Goodall 1).

In 2006, I was present for one of the most memorable wolf watching experiences in the history of Yellowstone National Park. Standing across the river was the Hayden Valley wolf pack's famous white wolf, alpha female 540F, accompanied by her pack and their five pups. 540F walked towards us, slinking out of the shadows to drink from the river; the whole time her eyes never left us. In those eyes I saw a powerful mysterious creature, but I also saw something almost human. The looming presence of fear and caution was unmistakable. Just as the ranchers fear for their business and family, a mother for her child, or even a hunter fearing the loss of his prey, this wolf feared for her pack. I saw a creature that was just as cautious as I was, not a monster. Wolves have emotions just like us, as explained in the words of Jane Goodall. She explains, "Not only are they highly intelligent, but they also have a rich emotional life, expressing feelings such as fear, anxiety, contentment, compassion and so on. They are intensely loyal to pack members and are likely to grieve over the death or disappearance of a close companion. And they certainly feel pain" (Goodall 3). Hunters and ranchers do not need the facts to accept the

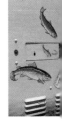

Public Rhetoric

wolf; they need the wisdom to see, to understand the other side of the story, and to acknowledge the importance of this majestic creature. The wolf is no monster, and it should not be portrayed as one by the media or any one else.

Jessica Hadley is an Art major.

Works Cited

Anderson, Dennis. "State's Wolves: Hunters to Hunted." *Star Tribune*. n.p., 12 Sept. 2012. Web. 03 Feb. 2014.

Berlin, Jay. "Would Real Wolves Act Like the Wolves of 'The Grey'?" *National Geographic*. n.p., 03 Feb. 2012. Web. 03 Feb. 2014.

Boyce, Joel. "Why We Will Boycott 'The Grey.'" *Care 2*. n.p., 27 Jan. 2012. Web. 03 Feb. 2014.

Chadwick, Douglas. "Wolf Wars." *National Geographic*. National Geographic Magazine, March 2010. Web. 19 Feb. 2014.

Goodall, Dr. Jane. "The Last Wolves." *The Washington Post*. n.p., 05 Jan. 2014. Web. 16 Feb. 2014.

Kaufman, Leslie. "After Years of Conflict, a New Dynamic in Wolf Country." *New York Times*. n.p. 04 Nov. 2011. Web. 24 Feb. 2014.

London, Jack. *White Fang*. New York: Scholastic, 1985. Print.

Nosowitz, Dan. "Stop Shooting Wolves, You Maniacs." *Popular Science*. n.p., 10 Dec. 2012. Web. 05 Feb. 2014.

Peterson, Laura. "Conflict Over Northern Rockies Delisting for Wolves Extends to Pacific Northwest." *New York Times*. n.p., 16 June 2011. Web. 21 Feb. 2014.

Tabish, Dillon. "Wolf Hunt Yields Higher Numbers." *Flathead Beacon*. Flathead Beacon, 27 Feb. 2013. Web. 21 Feb. 2014.

Toman, Eric. "Are Gray Wolves Endangered in the Northern Rocky Mountains? A Role for Social Science in Listing Determinations." *Bio Science*. 60.11 (Dec 2010): 941–948. Web. 26 Jan. 2014.

"The Last Wolf, 1943." *Yellowstone Science Magazine*. n.p., 1994. Web. 21 Feb. 2014.

"The War on Wolves." *Chicago Tribune*. n.p., 23 Sept. 2012. Web. 21 Feb. 2014.

CONSIDER THIS

- Addressing the counterargument (or opposing viewpoint) is a vital component of persuasion. Hadley discusses opposing views early in her essay. How would her argument change if she had structured her essay differently by presenting opposing views later?

- In what ways does the author use ethos, pathos, and logos to appeal to her audience? Can you identify specific passages that rely on each appeal?

- After considering their audience and purpose, writers must decide how to use first, second, and third person. In this essay, Hadley uses first person quite frequently. How would the tone of her essay—as well as her overall argument—shift if she had used third person instead?

The Translucent Culprit

Cammie Tolleshaug

The difference between a jellyfish and a plastic bag may not seem relevant to the average shopper reaching for something to hold her groceries. Yet for a sea turtle living just off of California's coastline, the difference between the two for his dinner could mean life or death. Most Americans do not think twice about accepting plastic bags from their grocery store clerk or about the disposal of all these bags; yet the accumulation of these flimsy, single-use items can build up much faster than expected. Although extremely handy, the convenience comes

LOOK HERE

For an alternative viewpoint on the use of plastic bags, go to **http://savetheplasticbag.com/**

at a price. Each bag has a much longer lifespan than its one time purpose of simply carrying vegetables from Albertson's to the fridge. From plastic production to decomposition, using a plastic bag for every purchase we make is taking a toll on the environment as well as our own health. Making a change is necessary, but how do we reconstruct a society that has come to revolve around ease? To start, San Luis Obispo adopted an ordinance in October 2012 that outlaws the distribution of plastic shopping bags for most retailers within county lines. These locations are also required to now charge a fee of at least five cents for every single-use paper bag a customer uses when checking out (Save). The point is to get shoppers in the habit of using reusable shopping bags. Some residents are onboard, while others debate whether or not making the switch is the best tactic for fixing the problem. Even though there might be some negative aspects, the ordinance to reinforce the use of reusable bags is overall beneficial to the county as well as society as a whole.

LOOK HERE

To learn more about the Great Pacific Garbage Patch, check out this documentary: **http://plasticparadisemovie.com**

Concerning the future of our planet, the fate of our ocean is in our hands, literally, when we carry a plastic shopping bag out of a store. Unfortunately, the destination of these man-made items usually ends in marine debris: pieces of garbage that have journeyed from land to sea by wind, storm drains, or directly dumped into the ocean. Ninety percent of marine debris is derived from plastics because of their tendency to float and their strong resistance to breaking down ("The Problem"). Overtime, the poor habits of people and the bags that aren't biodegradable have created a particular patch of garbage that is residing in the North

Pacific Subtropical Gyre. "Scientists have collected up to 750,000 bits of plastic in a single square kilometer (or 1.9 million bits per square mile) of the Great Pacific Garbage Patch." (Rutledge et al) The garbage spans an area comparable to the size of Texas, and it will continue to grow if humans continue to disregard disposal of the bags and other plastics they acquire. By halting the use of plastics in the first place, we nearly eliminate the fear of the ocean becoming increasingly concentrated with plastic debris. The "island" we've regretfully created is not the only concern either. Sometimes we forget that what lies under the surface is a whole ecosystem of life that is just as important as life on land. Sea turtles mistake plastic bags for jellyfish, one of their primary sources of food, and the result is an innocent turtle whose digestion has been compromised and may therefore starve to death or suffer poisoning from the toxins. Other animals die of ingesting the bags, as well as from entanglement in the marine debris. Supporters of plastic bags challenge claims made about marine pollution and question the amount of evidence available linking plastic bags to the distress of millions of sea creatures. According to the Coastal California Commission, there is enough evidence to prove that "plastic marine debris affects at least 267 species worldwide, including 86 percent of all sea turtle species, 44 percent of all sea bird species, and 43 percent of marine mammal species" ("The Problem"). The health of our oceans and its inhabitants is likely to improve with coastal counties such as San Luis Obispo undergoing changes regarding single-use plastic bags.

Plastic is not the only material that poses an environmental concern. Paper bags might seem like a great alternative for stores to hand out. They can be recycled, don't collect in oceans, and present far less harm to wildlife by improper disposal. However, they aren't the perfect solution for creating less pollution. Not only are they made of trees, a resource we need to conserve, but Save the Bag Coalition points out that paper bags generate, "significantly larger [greenhouse gas] emissions and result in greater atmospheric acidification, water consumption and ozone production than plastic bags" ("Save"). For this reason, the same ordinance that bans single-use plastic bags also includes a charge on paper ones. Hopefully by implementing a fee, residents will be more inclined to completely switch to bringing their own bags when shopping rather than paying for paper ones that contribute to environmental distress ("Save"). Long-term, the county's new policy is beneficial in minimizing waste of both plastic and paper bags.

Reusable shopping bags are a great alternative to plastic or paper bags. They provide the same convenience of carrying purchased goods from the store to the car, and from the car into your home, but without the worry of wasted materials or hassle of disposal afterwards. A reusable bag can be utilized for years and save hundreds of plastic bags from ending up in landfills, streets, or oceans. Also, reusable bags are produced more sustainably than plastic and by law contain fewer toxins. The main disadvantage to using your own bag is the inconvenience. Bob Cuddy, a writer for *The Tribune* of San Luis Obispo, illustrates a frequent

situation, "A shopper will grab her purse, lock her car and hurry into the grocery store thinking about bread, milk and other purchases. As she takes a few steps inside, she will stop abruptly, stand there like an exclamation point and mutter, 'Gosh darn it! I forgot my shopping bags'" (Cuddy). Remembering to bring your own bags is a struggle for many shoppers, and will continue to be, until new habits form. In the District of Columbia, the same law as the one San Luis Obispo acquired last year "caused as many as two-thirds of consumers to shift from single-use to reusable bags. After the District of Columbia law went into effect, there was a 50 percent decrease in the number of plastic bags found during an annual cleanup of the Anacostia River watershed" ("Save"). The hope is that in San Luis Obispo we will see similar results soon with a cleaner, less cluttered county. Surprisingly, even a small act such as using the same shopping bag for multiple purchases can have a large, positive impact on the community.

Repeatedly using fabric bags for groceries and other items solves several concerns for environment and wildlife well-being, but it may create a whole new issue in human health. Critics argue that re-usable bags can become breeding grounds for bacteria and illness if not properly washed. There have been documented cases of *E. coli* and food poisoning from use of contaminated bags, as well as contractions of the Norovirus. While this is a valid dilemma, there is a simple solution. These health risks can be eliminated with education on how to diligently wash and maintain the bags (Fletcher). The health hazards associated with plastic production are much greater. Chemicals in plastics, such as BPA and Pthalates, are absorbed through food and drinks in plastic containers or bags and measurable quantities can be detected in the bodies of over ninety percent of people. High amounts of these chemicals have been shown in studies to affect reproduction, brain development, alter hormones, and even increase the risk of heart disease and diabetes (Knoblauch). If the concern is disease or illness, plastics pose a much greater threat than re-usable bags. By focusing on the bigger picture, San Luis Obispo will reap more benefits than consequences from banning single-use plastic bags in grocery stores, pharmacies, convenience stores, and other retail locations.

The decision to make legislative changes regarding pollution regulation in San Luis Obispo affects more than just the county and its residents. For example, this particular ordinance has had a ripple effect along the West Coast as several other counties have adopted the same policies. In addition, backing the procedure with government authority forces everyone to change their behavior. Societies have no choice but to begin adjusting their lifestyles, and results will follow much sooner. Other towns across the United States may notice the success from eliminating plastic bags and eventually be convinced to instill the law nation-wide. Supporters of plastic bags criticize the effectiveness of the policy since plastic bags make up only about one percent of all litter. It is true that on a large scale this change would make miniscule progress in total environmental rehabilitation. However, even in California alone plastic bags exist in the billions and the majority of those are bound to end up in streets or waterways somewhere (Fletcher). It's all about perspective. In the end, it's worth making the effort even for a relatively small impact since it could potentially open the door for more opportunities and inspire others to be proactive. The county's adoption of this ordinance goes much further than relinquishing plastic bags in the local super-market—it's addressing the importance of our future.

Though there may be reasons to believe plastic bags are useful, the ends do not justify the means. The number of negative aspects regarding one-time use bags should make a customer think before saying "plastic is fine" to the cashier. San Luis Obispo, being a coastal county, is especially vulnerable to polluting oceans and beaches. It is a community that is responsible for the well being of its surroundings, and its residents are aware of their responsibility. The town in other ways has proven its concern about environmental wellness, too, by pro-viding a strong emphasis on recycling. Streets downtown are lined with bins decorated with a triangle of arrows and often overflowing with bottles and paper waste. Therefore, the atmosphere is one where citizens should feel connected and inspired to making a difference rather than focusing on luxury. A small change in our everyday lifestyle can result in a healthier planet, neighborhood, and gen-eration to come. And every bag counts—one less plastic bag in the ocean could mean the survival of one more sea turtle in the Pacific.

Cammie Tolleshaug is a Nutrition major.

Works Cited

Cuddy, Bob. "Controversial bag ban panned and praised." *The Tribune* 31 December 2012. Web.

Fletcher, Jaimee Lynn and Joanna Clay. "Both Sides of Bag Ban Seek a Clear Look." *The Orange County Register* 16 February 2013. Web.

Knoblauch, Jessica A. "The Environmental Toll of Plastics." *Environmental Health News*. Environmental Health Sciences, 2 July 2009. Web. October 2013.

Rutledge, Kim, et al. "Great Pacific Garbage Patch." *Education Beta*. Ed. Kara West and Jeannie Evers. *National Geographic*, 2013. Web. 9 November 2013.

"Save the Plastic Bag Coalition vs. County of Marin. No. A133868." *PlasticBagLaws.org*. n.p., 25 July 2013. Web. 16 November 2013.

"The Problem With Marine Debris." *California Coastal Commission*. State of California, 2013. Web. 16 November 2013.

CONSIDER THIS

- Most of us know that plastic bags pollute the environment, so how does this writer create an argument with an almost absent "opposition" voice? In other words, is it clear from the outset that residents of San Luis Obispo County are enraged by this ordinance? Is there anything you could suggest to make this argument even more compelling?

- Do you think this argument would have been stronger had the writer offered more compelling evidence about the effects of plastics on sea turtles and other marine life since she often alludes to the effects plastics have on them?

- Does Tolleshaug offer enough supporting evidence for her argument: personal/expert testimony, statistics, facts, examples, anecdotes, analogies, history?

Fracking: The Big Bad Monster?

Gordon Belyea

I don't care what Dunkin' Donuts tries to preach: America does not run on donuts— America runs on oil and natural gas. Commonly abbreviated as "fracking," horizontal hydro-fracturing extracts natural gas from underground. This increasingly common method is implemented when gas would be difficult, if not impossible, to extract using conventional methods, such as oilrig drilling. Even though fracking has just recently become a large contributor to America's oil production and extraction, the technology has existed for much longer (Merrill 972). The rise in the use of fracking has become a hot news topic for many reasons. Opponents of fracking insist the environmental implications overbear any positives associated with it, but I aim to investigate what benefits exist using this technique and whether or not it may be as bad as the public perceives it to be.

For decades, petroleum engineers sought a way to retrieve the gas trapped in the earth. In conventional drilling, a vertical pipe is drilled from the surface to an oil or gas reservoir in the ground. When the pipe penetrates into the reservoir, the pressure from the rock and soil above cause the oil or gas to flow through the pipe and up to the surface (Merrill 971). The process is easy because the oil or gas is pressurized from the natural subsurface environment, and the petroleum industry has been extracting crude oil for over 100 years this way. However, not all the gas and oil below us lies in these underground deposits. Frequently, the gas to be extracted lies in shale deposits thousands of feet below the surface. This is where fracking comes in. Fracking companies pump high-pressure hydraulic fluid into these permeable layers of earth, forcing the gas out the shale. This fractures the shale and releases the gas trapped inside. The depth from which the gas is extracted is called the "pit," or the well's source of water for the fracking operation.

Elizabeth Kolbert, in her article for the *New Yorker*, explains that until the last twelve or so years the technique was not economic or efficient enough to use on a large scale. But due to "advances in drilling technology, extracting the gas [has become] a lucrative proposition" (Kolbert). This lucrative proposition has helped to spawn the widespread use of fracking. Fracking has been called a "new-aged gold rush" and an "Energy Renaissance" by Lesley Stahl of *60 Minutes*. She reported, "some ten thousand wells are to be drilled in some of the poorest areas of the United States" (Stahl). Shale gas is abundant in the United

> **LOOK HERE**
>
> To see a map illustrating where shale gas is found in the United States, go to:
>
> **http://energy.gov/sites/prod/files/2013/04/ f0/where_is_shale_gas_found.pdf**

States. The owners of the land where the drilling takes place are "often impoverished farmers who can become overnight millionaires" called Shaleionaires (Stahl). Energy companies lease the rights to drill from the owners of the land. This stimulates the local economy and helps all those in it.

Thomas Merrill, a professor at Colombia Law School, has written extensively about property law, administrative law, and environmental law. Merrill cited that the sudden increase in fracking created a rapid expansion of reserves in the United States, which in turn created many jobs in the oil and gas extraction industries. In his paper, "Four Questions About Fracking," published by the Case Western Reserve Law Review, he admitted, "exactly how many more jobs is guesswork." But he cites that "President Obama, in his 2012 State of the Union address, said 600,000" could be added due to fracking (Merrill 972). Moreover, Merrill explains the significance of this in a recovering economy. "The unemployment rate in North Dakota, where oil production using fracking technology is booming, is 3.7 percent, less than half the national average" (Merrill 973). Fracking not only helps those who own the land but also helps the community where it takes place. Fracking provides jobs not only in the industries immediately involved in it, but also in all the support, service, entertainment, and other industries that flow in with the gas.

Increased oil reserves can also be part of a solution for peace in the Middle East. The United States is so heavily dependent on foreign oil that it often times dictates foreign policy. Only a few short years ago, the globe was on edge, waiting to see what would happen in the standoff between Iran

LOOK HERE

For further information on fracking, visit the *Gasland* website:
http://www.gaslandthemovie.com

and the United Nations. Iran was unyielding about building uranium enrichment facilities. Iran openly tested missiles capable hitting of numerous intercontinental targets, such as Israel. Denver Nicks, for *Time*, wrote, "the difference [between then and now], according to former Obama administration National Security Advisor Tom Donilon, can be summed up in one word: "fracking" (Nicks). Nicks also wrote that Donilon correlated "a direct line between the U.S.-led sanctions effort to put pressure on Iran and the flood of oil and gas coming out of the ground at home due to fracking technology" (Nicks). The United States held harsh sanctions against Iran, effectively closing them out of trade with the world. This crippled their economy. Iran saw "a reduction in the ability to sell oil, pressure on their currency, high inflation, high unemployment, the inability to do any real financing within the marketplace. And that led directly, I think, to the election of Rouhani last spring" (Nicks). After they "saw the writing on the wall" Iran turned itself around and began talks about dismantling their

nuclear program. America, once heavily dependent on foreign oil, could not have survived these sanctions on Iran without the influx of domestic oil and gas. The United States now has access to the reserves it needs domestically to not be so heavily dependent on major petroleum exporting nations. This provides leverage for the United States that we did not previously have. Imagine that. No need for wars over oil or harmful interventions by us anymore. We can solve our problems diplomatically and effectively with the help of fracking.

Many people in the United States believe that fracking is incredibly harmful to humans or the environment. According to Merrill's article, "fracking fluid contains a small percentage of chemicals, some of which, like arsenic, are known toxics and others of which, like benzene, are known carcinogens. If these chemicals find their way into the groundwater, they could pose a health risk" (Merrill 981). Joe Hoffman, in his article for Carleton College, states, "storage of the wastewater is currently under the regulatory jurisdiction of states, many of whom have weak to nonexistent policies protecting the environment" (Hoffman). In addition, Hoffman argues that these procedures are not currently adequate to protect the environment. I agree with Hoffman and suggest that we regulate the use, control, and disposal of fracking fluid. So how often are spills due to fracking?

My father, Richard Belyea, a registered professional hydro-geologist, has worked in the oil industry. Currently he works as an environmental banker, assessing groundwater and subsurface soil contamination and providing loans to customers to clean up their mess. Mr. Belyea believes that "like any industry, there have been a few 'bad actors,' companies that have cut corners and not adequately cemented the pipe casing" (Belyea). When drilling for natural gas, companies are required to encase their bore in cement to block seepage of fracking fluid or natural gas into the soil or groundwater; however some do not do this well, causing natural gas to trickle into groundwater reserves utilized by the public. He argues that in reality "these incidences have been few and far between and sensationalized by the media" (Belyea). In fact, Susan Brantley, a professor of Geological Sciences at Penn State, cited in an article for the *New York Times* that:

> In one study of two hundred private water wells in the fracking regions of Pennsylvania, water quality was the same before and soon after drilling in all wells except one. The only surprise from that study was that many of the wells failed drinking water regulations before drilling started. (2)

With fracking, like most new technology, there is the fear of the unknown or of the new. Sometimes this fear is over exaggerated and is reflected in many of the criticisms of fracking. One critique of fracking I can get behind is its excessive use of water. Belyea stated, "the drilling and hydraulic fracturing through use of a

horizontal shale gas may typically require 2–4 million gallons of water" (Belyea). According to an article originally published by Bloomberg and reprinted in the *Carlsbad Current*, a newspaper in New Mexico, in 2012, fracking consumed some 50 billion gallons of water ("Thirst"). California and much of the west is currently facing a debilitating drought, making this use of water seem quite excessive. However, as reported in NPR's State Impact series, Canadian company GasFrac uses a process that does not "use any water" (Galbraith). The gel they use evaporates underground "eliminating the risk of contamination" writes *Time* in its Top 25

LOOK HERE

For more expert perspectives on fracking, check out the five interviews available at the Switch Energy Project's website:

http://www.switchenergyproject.com/topics/fracking

inventions of 2013 ("Waterless"). While I admit that conventional fracking's use of water is gluttonous, the use of GasFrac's method could potentially solve two of the major problems typically associated with fracking, water use and contamination.

Through my studies as a mechanical engineering student, I understand the importance of fracking as a crucial way for extracting energy resources. As a mechanical engineer, I could work in the automotive or aerospace industries, designing machines that run on fuels distilled and refined by oil companies. I could even work in the petroleum industry itself; either onsite in the field, designing componentry dealing with any aspect of the extraction, production, storage, or transportation of hydrocarbon based fossil fuels. Right now, the automotive and aerospace industries rely on oil and gas, but they are working towards a broader energy use. To keep commerce, transportation, and our way of life flowing, for the meantime, we need oil.

Unfortunately, fossil fuel use will not end overnight. While options focusing on renewable resources, which currently only represents 13% of electricity production (such as wind, solar, water, geothermal, and others), will be implemented in the future (Belyea), we as a society will rely on petroleum-based products for many years to come. We can also not phase out the current technologies we depend on immediately, and while we move towards greener technologies, society must look towards cleaner, sustainable, and local ways of producing the energy required. Innovations like GasFrac's gel are what we need to keep striving towards in our pursuit of clean technologies. Fracking would be a part of a broad strategy working alongside the growing use of wind, solar, water, and nuclear. Nothing is perfect, but fracking is a good option for America's energy needs now.

Gordon Belyea is a Mechanical Engineering major.

Works Cited

Belyea, Richard. Personal Interview. 25 Feb. 2014.

Brantley, Susan L., and Anna Meyendoroff. "The Facts on Fracking." *International Herald Tribune*: 10. Mar. 14 2013. ProQuest. Web. 27 Feb. 2014.

"Editorial: States must Contain Fracking's Enormous Thirst for Water." *Carlsbad Current.* Argus. Feb. 22 2014. ProQuest. Web. 5 Mar. 2014.

Galbraith, Kate. "Waterless Fracking Makes Headway in Texas, Slowly." *NPR State Impact/Texas Tribune.* NPR, 27 Mar. 2013. Web. 03 Mar. 2014.

Hoffman, Joe. "Potential Health and Environmental Effects of Hydrofracking in the Williston Basin, Montana." *Geology and Human Health.* College of Carleton, 13 Sept. 2013. Web. 28 Feb. 2014.

Kolbert, Elizabeth. "Burning Love." *The New Yorker.* The New Yorker, 05 Dec. 2011. Web. 05 Mar. 2014.

Merrill, Thomas W. "Four Questions About Fracking." *Case Western Reserve Law Review* 63.4 (2013): 971–993. Academic Search Premier. Web. 19 Feb. 2014.

Nicks, Denver. "How the U.S. Energy Boom Is Changing America's Place in the World." *Time.* Time Magazine, 8 Feb. 2014. Web. 18 Feb. 2014.

Stahl, Lesley. "Shale Gas Drilling: Pros & Cons." *60 Minutes.* CBS. New York, NY, 14 Nov. 2010. Television.

"Waterless Fracking: The 25 Best Inventions of the Year." *Time.* Time Magazine, 13 Nov. 2013. Web. 03 Mar. 2014.

CONSIDER THIS

- Belyea includes testimony from his father, a hydro-geologist. Does such a choice enhance his ethos? Or, does integrating evidence based on an interview with his father suggest that this writer might have a bias on the subject? How should a writer's biases be addressed in an argument?

- Opponents of fracking cite flammable water as a compelling enough reason to question the effectiveness of this method of gas extraction. In fact, there are videos readily available online that display homeowners turning on their kitchen faucets and lighting a match in the flowing water. The writer of this essay does not address this issue. Had he done so, how would your stance on the subject transform? Do you think it was wise to avoid this aspect of the argument?

- At one point in the essay, Belyea admits that he agrees with one of the arguments against fracking. What point does he agree with, and how does his validation of the point augment his credibility?

- As you read through this essay, did you notice the tone the writer opens and closes with? Does his use of first and second person improve or weaken his argument?

The Media Today

Jon Kuzmich

Have you ever watched the news on an unfamiliar station only to recoil in disgust from the blatantly false dribble that the newscasters spewed from their mouths, and then proceeded to rant about how they must be fools or insane to believe what they had just said? You probably haven't reacted that extremely to opposing views, but most everyone has, at some point in their lives, acted aversely to information or opinions that contradict their beliefs. This aversion to conflicting beliefs is due to a psychological phenomenon called cognitive dissonance, and it seems to plague viewer's thoughts on the content of media ("Cognitive Dissonance"; Claussen 213). But then why do news stations such as FOX News, CNN, and MSNBC offer biased news that produce cognitive dissonance in some viewers? Journalistic entities, like news stations and other sources of information, should report the news objectively and in its entirety, regardless of political standing and without opinionated responses geared towards certain ideologies.

News stations haven't always added an ideological spin on the news, though. According to Shanto Iyengar of Stanford University and Kyu S. Hahn of UCLA, forty years ago most Americans received their news through a few networks. These networks used a "point-counterpoint" method of reporting news. Technological advances since then, like cable television and the Internet, have allowed for a competitive news media environment that fosters partisan news reporting (Iyengar and Hahn 20). This, in turn, allows people to selectively expose themselves to information that is consistent and resonates with their beliefs or preferences.

The biased, partisan reporting of the media can mislead voters by suppressing information. Media outlets suppressing information on key issues lead voters to make electoral decisions by shaping false beliefs in voters (Bernhardt, Krasa, and Polborn 1092). Think of all of the political mistakes that may have been caused due to some key issue of a political policy being left

> ## LOOK HERE
>
> Check out these side-by-side comparisons of opinion vs. factual reporting on the major news networks:
>
> http://stateofthemedia.org/2013/special-reports-landing-page/the-changing-tv-news-landscape/

out of a broadcast, influencing public opinion, and affecting how people vote. If news networks reported objectively with the "point-counterpoint" method of reporting that old networks employed, some of those mistakes would have been avoided.

Why then do media outlets suppress information that could prevent a blunder on a national scale? Media outlets actually benefit by providing voters with skewed information. By appealing to the beliefs of their viewers through left-biased or right-biased news, media outlets maximize their profits by attracting more viewers than they would if they reported unbiased, objective news (Bernhardt, Krasa, and Polborn 1095). The radio talk show host Rush Limbaugh even stated that "[his] real purpose is to attract the largest audience [he] can, and hold it for as long as [he] can, so [he] can charge confiscatory advertising rates" (qtd. in Bernhardt, Krasa, and Polborn 1098). Limbaugh and other news network anchors pander to the beliefs of their audience for profit despite the possibility of causing electoral mistakes that affect the entire nation. This kind of selfish, for-profit behavior manipulates the population and can polarize them to extremes.

Political elites, such as congressman and other politicians, have already become more polarized into separate ideologies, paralleling the growth of partisan messages being broadcasted in the media over the last 25 years (Prior 103). However, there is not enough evidence to suggest that the majority of Americans have fallen victim to attitude polarization from these partisan messages, despite an increase in partisan voting patterns. The evidence that the politically engaged have become more partisan is stronger, though, hinting at political polarization among an influential minority (Prior 103). Over time, if news networks continue to broadcast partisan messages and viewers listen, they are in danger of incorporating such messages into their viewers' beliefs and encouraging viewers to make uninformed decisions that may cause electoral mistakes.

Viewers already select which news networks they receive their information from, while avoiding others, affecting their political standing from the partisan messages they receive. In an experiment to see how viewers favored certain news outlets but not others based on their political standing, it was found that most Republicans converged to FOX News and avoided left-leaning news sources, such as CNN and NPR. Conversely, Democrats avoided FOX News, but didn't favor any particular news source (Iyengar, Hahn 30). The headlines of the articles for each source were the same. The only difference between the articles was the news source, yet Democrats and Republicans opted to read the articles from a news source they thought shared their political beliefs. The unconscious drive to avoid contradictory information prevents them from choosing contradictory news sources. If these sources suppressed such contradictory information, both Democrats and Republicans would be oblivious to key issues pertaining to political policies, causing misunderstanding on both sides. By only consuming news from biased news sources, they are more likely to refuse to acknowledge alternative views and remain committed to their own.

The biases present in news media, causing this polarization, are becoming more apparent to Americans and are thus causing a hostile outlook on biased

media. "Only 29% of Americans say news organizations get their facts straight and 18% say media deal fairly with all sides of political issues, low points in these trends since 1985" (Arceneaux, Johnson, and Murphy 174). Viewers are also able to recognize the ideological biases of information sources. In a comparison of FOX News, CNN, and Comedy Central's *The Daily Show*, people identified the political leaning of each source accurately (Arceneaux, Johnson, and Murphy 174). This increased perception of bias in media may be due to how people have begun to perceive the media in a more hostile light. Hopefully the recognition of partisan media outlets will force change for more objective news networks that abstain from biased reporting and encourage those that are currently doing so.

Until the change to objective reporting happens, the partisan messages of biased media still reach the American public, affecting their beliefs and voting behavior. During the 2004 presidential election and after the United States invaded Iraq under the Bush administration, most Americans still had false beliefs

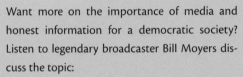

LOOK HERE

Want more on the importance of media and honest information for a democratic society? Listen to legendary broadcaster Bill Moyers discuss the topic:

http://www.democracynow.org/2008/6/9/moyers

about the Iraq War, stemming from the media bias from their respective news sources (Bernhardt, Krasa, and Polborn 1092). Those that watched FOX News were more likely to support Bush 70% to 21% and were more likely to believe that Saddam Hussein had links to Al-Qaeda, supported the 9/11 attacks, and possessed

weapons of mass destruction (Bernhardt, Krasa, and Polborn 1092). The effect was opposite for those who received most of their information from CNN. They were more likely to support Kerry 67% to 26% and believe that Saddam Hussein did not have links to Al-Qaeda, support the 9/11 attacks, or possess weapons of mass destruction. The 2004 election was decided by just 2.5% in the popular vote, Bush being the winner 50.73% to Kerry's 48.27% ("Federal Elections 2004"). What would have happened if FOX News and CNN reported uniformly and the vast differences in beliefs of the Iraq War were stabilized? Bush may have lost the 2004 election to Kerry, and our country's direction may have been altered drastically. The troops in Iraq may have been recalled, and the war may have ended much sooner than 2011, preventing thousands of casualties.

The polarized political elite can abuse the effect of partisan media to their advantage to sway voters to vote a certain way. The media is often a battleground for politicians warring over the public opinion of their constituents. In the most recent presidential election President Obama employed the partisan media to

discredit his opponent Mitt Romney. Sid Bedingfield and Dien Anshari identified the ways in which he did so: The Obama team identified five negative frames that they wanted to emphasize in advertising and embed in news media. They intended to undermine Romney's image as a successful businessman who understood how the economy worked by claiming that he had failed to create jobs as governor of Massachusetts, and that his firm, Bain Capital, had destroyed companies and shipped jobs abroad. They focused on his wealth, claiming that he was out of touch with middle-class voters and had avoided paying his fair share of taxes. Finally, they also claimed that Romney's policies would hurt women.

Obama went on to win the 2012 presidential election by 4% more of the popular vote than Romney ("2012 Presidential Popular"). His use of partisan messages in the media may have influenced enough swing voters to win him the election. This shows how powerful of a tool news media is to political elites that wish to manipulate voters into supporting their policies. Objective news sources couldn't be used to manipulate because they must detail both sides of every story, like whether or not Romney's policies would hurt women, or if he dodged his taxes.

Biased reporting and the suppression of information by journalistic entities must stop. They manipulate how the public sees reality and disregard the consequences. Their reason for this manipulation isn't even to control how Americans vote; it's merely a side-effect of the partisan messages they broadcast to attract viewers that wish to reaffirm their beliefs. The media's reasons for misleading the public is purely based upon profit, and by doing so, they enable others that want to control the voting behaviors of Americans. All of this can be avoided in the future by fostering an environment where it is beneficial to take an objective stance on political issues, without suppressing important, key details. Should Americans live in a nation where the population is manipulated through deceit, or a nation where one can be informed from any news network without being disgusted or deceived?

Jon Kuzmich is a Computer Science major.

Works Cited

Arceneaux, Kevin, Martin Johnson, and Chad Murphy. "Polarized Political Communication, Oppositional Media Hostility, and Selective Exposure." *Journal of Politics* 74.1 (2012): 174–186. Academic Search Premier. Web. 22 Feb. 2014.

Bedingfield, Sid, and Dien Anshari. "Thinking About Romney: Frame Building in a Battleground State in the 2012 Presidential Election." *Journalism & Mass Communication Quarterly* 91.1 (2014): 78–97. Academic Search Premier. Web. 22 Feb. 2014.

Bernhardt, Dan, Stefan Krasa, and Mattias Polborn. "Political Polarization and the Electoral Effects of Media Bias." *Journal of Public Economics* 92.5-6 (2008): 1092–1104. Print.

"Cognitive Dissonance." *ScienceDaily*. ScienceDaily, n.d. Web. 19 Feb. 2014.

Claussen, D. S. "Cognitive Dissonance, Media Illiteracy, and Public Opinion on News Media." *American Behavioral Scientist* 48.2 (2004): 212–18. Print.

"Federal Elections 2004." *Federal Election Commission*. United States Government, May 2005. Web. 22 Feb. 2014.

Iyengar, Shanto, and Kyu S. Hahn. "Red Media, Blue Media: Evidence of Ideological Selectivity in Media Use." *Journal of Communication* 59.1 (2009): 19–39. Academic Search Premier. Web. 19 Feb. 2014.

Prior, Markus. "Media and Political Polarization." *Annual Review of Political Science* 16 (2013): 101–127. Academic Search Premier. Web. 18 Feb. 2014.

"2012 Presidential Popular Vote Summary." Federal Election Commission. United States Government, 06 Nov. 2012. Web. 22 Feb. 2014.

CONSIDER THIS

- In order for an argument to be effective, the rhetorician can take advantage of a moment's kairos (the timeliness and relevancy of an issue). Can you think of a current issue that, if integrated into this essay, might help further establish the argument's kairos?

- To reach the widest audience, a rhetorician needs to approach an argument from a balanced perspective. How does Kuzmich's tone and use of bipartisan examples contribute to the effectiveness of the argument?

Appendices

Look to the appendices for information on:

- Campus Resources (i.e., The University Writing and Rhetoric Center, Disability Resource Center, Kennedy Library)
- Avoiding Plagiarism
- General Education Course Objectives
- The Graduation Writing Requirement
- Submitting your work to next year's *Fresh Voices*

Mustang Pride
Photograph by Carlos Giron

Artist's Note: Mustangs are strong, intelligent animals. They are also independent, high-spirited animals that can endure many obstacles that come their way. As such, a mustang is the perfect mascot for Cal Poly, SLO: our students are strong, intelligent, independent individuals who stand tall and confident, like a Mustang.

Appendices

Campus Resources: Where to Find Help

YOUR INSTRUCTOR'S OFFICE HOURS

If you are struggling to understand a concept studied in class or are simply having a hard time choosing a topic for an essay, do not hesitate to meet with your instructor during his/her designated office hours (or make an appointment if those hours don't work with your schedule). Your instructor's office hours will be posted in the course syllabus.

First-year students are often too intimidated or anxious to meet one-on-one with their instructors, yet a short meeting with your instructor can make a major difference when it comes to being successful in a course. Do not wait until you receive low grades on an essay or feel overwhelmed in the course before asking for help. Your instructor will appreciate you taking a pro-active stance toward your own development as a writer. Make it a point to ask for assistance when you need it.

DISABILITY RESOURCE CENTER

If you have been diagnosed with a learning disability, or are concerned that you may have an undiagnosed disability that is affecting your academic performance, contact Cal Poly's Disability Resource Center for further assistance (http://drc.calpoly.edu/).

SUPPORT FOR ENGLISH AS A SECOND LANGUAGE STUDENTS

The Cal Poly Composition Program is committed to placing students into writing courses that will best support them. Students for whom English is a second (or even third) language may want to consider taking writing classes that are intended to address their needs and talents (ENGL 113, 133).

To decide if such a writing course will benefit you, please consider the following:

- Do you speak a language other than English at home?
- Do your parents speak a language other than English at home?
- Did your previous instructors suggest that you might benefit from second-language support?
- Do you struggle when reading long, complex texts that are written in English?

If you are interested in taking a course that supports second-language students, please see the description of ENGL 133 later in this appendix.

Or, if you would like to work with a tutor who is trained to support students for whom English is not their first language, please contact the University Writing and Rhetoric Center (see next section).

THE UNIVERSITY WRITING AND RHETORIC CENTER

The University Writing and Rhetoric Center (UWRC) offers *free,* one-to-one consultations for *any class project* that requires an element of writing and rhetoric: reading, writing, speaking, and developing visual texts. Tutors are undergraduate and graduate students professionally trained both in a 300-level course on one-to-one conferencing and in subsequent workshops on writing and rhetoric in the disciplines. Tutors are available to help all Cal Poly students improve their writing skills.

Students may use the UWRC's services at any stage of the writing process, whether they are getting started on a project or editing at the final stages. All writers are welcome.

The Center serves students at three locations on campus:
- **Building 10, Room 138**
- **Kennedy Library, Room 202B**
- **The study lounge in Trinity Hall**

Thirty-minute and sixty-minute sessions are available by appointment or on a first-come, first-served basis.

To schedule a session with a writing consultant, go to

www.calpoly.mywconline.com

Writing and Rhetoric Center tutors are prepared to assist you with the following:

- Understanding the expectations of an assignment
- Brainstorming and generating ideas
- Generating and organizing your ideas
- Clarifying your purpose
- Developing and supporting your argument
- Researching and documenting sources
- Adhering to a specific format, such as MLA or APA
- Reviewing grammar and punctuation
- Writing in all disciplines (e.g., lab reports, research papers, technical reports)
- Completing senior projects
- Preparing for the Writing Proficiency Exam (WPE)

Keep in mind that the Center's tutors do not simply proofread papers or provide students with a stamp of approval on an assignment. Instead, the goal of a tutoring session is to help students gain new writing strategies and improve their writing skills so that they more successfully may complete writing tasks at Cal Poly and beyond.

Right Here. Write Now!

Dear Student:

As Director of the University Writing & Rhetoric Center, I can assure you that my office is committed to supporting you as you move through your writing experiences at Cal Poly. In particular, if you have any questions or concerns about satisfying the GWR, please do not hesitate to contact my office at 756-2067 or writingcenter@calpoly.edu. The Writing and Rhetoric Center tutors and I are excited to see you in the center. Remember, all writers are welcome! Stop by and see us often.

Kennedy Library: Resources for English 133/134

Personal Help in Kennedy Library

Research Help Desk—Room 111: Get in-person help from a LibRAT, specially-trained Cal Poly students who know how to help you find what you are looking for. LibRATs are very friendly and don't bite!

Phone Support: If you prefer to speak to someone, call 756-2649.

Chat Help: Offered by LibRATs, librarians and Kennedy Library staff.

For help hours, information about the chat box, go to: http://lib.calpoly.edu/ask/

Research Resources

As a Cal Poly student, you have access to some very extensive resources and you should take advantage of them while you can. Now is your chance to move beyond Wikipedia.

Books

PolyCAT helps you locate books, journals, DVDs and more in Kennedy Library, available immediately.

Link+ helps you locate books and other materials in Kennedy and 50 other libraries. They will arrive at the library for pick-up in 3–5 days.

Articles

For the list of Most Useful Databases, go to: Kennedy Home Page > Articles > Most Useful Databases.

This list includes several databases useful for English 133/134 under headings that suggest their particular usefulness. These databases often include full-text articles. If you don't see PDF or HTML when you see a good article, click the **Find It** button, as this may lead you to the full text in another database. Most databases allow you to email yourself articles and citations. Some let you select for peer-reviewed results.

Research Guides

English 134: links to catalogs, databases, and resources relevant to this course.

Freshmen 101: general introduction to the library, designed in part for English 133/134. It also includes a tutorial on the research process.

Online Citation Help

Citation examples based on MLA 7th edition are available online at: http://lib.calpoly.edu/research/citations/mla.html

The MLA 7th edition is available at the Research Help Desk and at the Circulation (front) desk, call number LB2369 .G53 2009.

The OWL at Purdue provides excellent MLA examples and aid: http://owl.english.purdue.edu/owl/resource/747/01/

You can also seek individual help with citation at the **Research Help Desk, Room 111**.

Key Research Vocabulary for English 133/134

Abstract: a brief description of the contents of an article.

Citation: information about a book or article that minimally includes author, title, date, and publisher.

Citation style: there are many formats for citation, such as MLA, Chicago, APA, etc. English 134 uses MLA.

Call Number: Library of Congress classification codes. The unique combination of letters and numbers tells you where a book is found among similar items. To find which floor your book is on, look at a library map.

Peer-Reviewed Journal: a journal that publishes articles only after they have been subjected to critique by multiple scholars in that field. Signs that an article is peer-reviewed are the presence of many citations, a text-heavy appearance, and academic affiliations of the editors and authors. If you are uncertain, one way to be sure is to visit the home page of the journal. Peer-reviewed journals are usually proud of the fact and announce it there.

Plagiarism: not giving proper credit for information to its source; copying someone else's ideas and passing them off as your own. In other words, don't cut and paste, or paraphrase, without giving credit.

For other information about the Library, use the Kennedy Home Page quick search box, and select for Website Content. http://lib.calpoly.edu/

This section was contributed by Brett Bodemer,
Humanities and Social Sciences Librarian at Robert E. Kennedy Library.

Defining and Avoiding Plagiarism

Cal Poly and the English Department prohibit cheating or academic dishonesty in any form.

DEFINING PLAGIARISM

Cal Poly's Campus Administrative Manual 684.3 states:

> "Plagiarism is defined as the act of using the ideas or work of another person or persons as if they were one's own without giving proper credit to the source. Such an act is not plagiarism if it is ascertained that the ideas were arrived through independent reasoning or logic or where the thought or idea is common knowledge. Acknowledgement of an original author or source must be made through appropriate references; i.e., quotation marks, footnotes, or commentary. Examples of plagiarism include, but are not limited to the following: the submission of a work, either in part or in whole completed by another; failure to give credit for ideas, statements, facts or conclusions which rightfully belong to another; failure to use quotation marks when quoting directly from another, whether it be a paragraph, a sentence, or even a part thereof; close and lengthy paraphrasing of another's writing without credit or originality; use of another's project or programs or part thereof without giving credit."

In other words, plagiarism occurs when, without proper citation, you quote a source's words exactly, use images or audio files created by someone else, or restate a source's ideas in your own words. Submitting a paper that you have written for another class (including work written for your high school classes) without the knowledge or permission of your instructors could result in penalty. Purchasing or downloading essays is also a form of plagiarism since the work you hand in is not your own.

You may have previously learned "rules" which tell you that you don't need to use quotation marks or to cite your sources unless you "borrow" multiple consecutive words, which isn't accurate. Anytime you use words and ideas that are not your own, you will be expected to cite the source.

EXAMPLES OF PLAGIARISM

- The submission of another person's work in any medium, either in part or as a whole, without acknowledgement
- Failure to give credit for ideas, statements, facts, or conclusions that rightfully belong to another person
- Failure to use quotation marks when quoting directly from another source whether the quotation is a paragraph, a sentence, or a phrase

- Paraphrasing (putting in your own words) another person's work without acknowledging that person as the author
- Including images, chart, graphs, etc., in your essay without properly citing the original source material (i.e., Google images)
- Submitting your written work for another class unless you have the express permission of both instructors

Note that quotation marks, signal phrases, and parenthetical citations generally address these problems.

READING *FRESH VOICES* ESSAYS THAT CITE SOURCES

As you read the essays in this collection, focus on how students use sources to support their own ideas. In particular, note how they introduce and quote sources, how they paraphrase, summarize, and integrate quotations with signal phrases. In addition, don't skip over the works cited page at the end of essays. Rather, focus on how this page supplements the essay: every source cited in the essay (including images) needs to appear here. Learning how to incorporate and cite sources properly helps to build your credibility (*ethos*) with your readers. While you may learn a different citation style in your major (MLA, APA, Chicago, etc.), the key is to learn how to work with outside sources. Once you understand the basic principles for incorporating source material, you will be able to adapt to any citation style.

THE CONSEQUENCES

According to university policy, as a student at Cal Poly, you are responsible for your actions. English 134 instructors have clearly stated plagiarism policies on their syllabi. **It is your responsibility to become familiar with the plagiarism policies in your classes.**

Upon discovery of any form of academic dishonesty, you will be subject to a penalty as determined by the instructor (you may fail the assignment; you may fail the entire course). In addition, a report detailing the incident of academic dishonesty, as well as the course's penalty, will be filed with the Office of Student Rights and Responsibilities.

According to the Office of Student Rights and Responsibilities, "Cheating requires, at a minimum, an 'F' assigned to the assignment, exam, or task, and this 'F' must be reflected in the course grade. The instructor may assign an 'F' course grade for an incidence of cheating."

Work Cited
"Plagiarism." Office of Student Rights and Responsibilities. Consulted 17 June 2012. <http://www.osrr.calpoly.edu/plagiarism/>.

General Education Course Objectives

The General Education Course Objectives for English 133 and 134 state that as a student enrolled in the course, you will learn to:

1. Understand the writing act as a means of exploring and expressing your ideas.

2. Approach the act of writing as a recursive process that includes drafting, revising, editing and proofreading.

3. Develop and apply a rhetorical awareness of your audience and use that awareness to assess your audiences and adjust your utterances to that audience.

4. Understand major organizational strategies and apply those strategies effectively with reference to your audiences.

5. Become aware of the major stylistic options such as voice, tone, figurative language and point of view and apply these options with rhetorical appropriateness.

6. Apply the above objectives so as to write essays that are unified, coherent, and free of significant grammar, usage, punctuation, mechanics, and spelling errors.

7. Read critically in such a way as to understand and to derive rhetorical principles and tactics that you can apply in writing and in critical reading of other students' papers.

8. Apply all of the above principles to in- and out-of-class original writing of not fewer than **4,000 words.**

English 133 and 134 emphasize a process approach to composition: instructors will engage in a dialogue with you about your writing, providing feedback designed to prompt you to rethink your work. You will gain competence as a writer by learning how to assess your own work. In addition, English 133 and 134 are rhetorically oriented, which means you will learn to account for the relationship between writer, reader, and text when you write.

Composition at Cal Poly:
Catalog Course Descriptions

The following courses constitute the composition curriculum at Cal Poly.

ENGL 102 Basic Writing II (4) (CR/NC)

Instruction in the writing process. Practice in the strategies of writing, revising, and editing paragraphs and essays with attention paid to focus, support, and organization. Directed readings of exemplary prose. Not for baccalaureate credit. Credit/No Credit grading only. Repeatable. 4 lectures. **Next Course in Sequence:** ENGL 134

ENGL 113 Essay Writing/ESL (4) (CR/NC)

Practice in essay writing with special attention paid to the writing process. Focus on using details and examples for effective development. Review of grammar problems specific to ESL students. Journal writing to enhance fluency. Directed readings of essays and fiction. Not for baccalaureate credit. Credit/No Credit grading only. 4 lectures. **Prerequisite:** ENGL 111 or ENGL 112, or consent of instructor. **Next Course in Sequence:** ENGL 133

> **Note:** All ENGL 102 and 113 courses have been "stretched," which means that students in these courses continue to work with the same group of students and the same instructor in ENGL 133/134.

ENGL 103 Writing Laboratory (1) (CR/NC)

Directed practice in writing in a laboratory environment. Required of all students scoring below 147 on the English Placement Test (EPT). Not for baccalaureate credit. Credit/No Credit grading only. To be taken concurrently with the ENGL 133 and 134 parts of the stretch sequences.

ENGL 133 Writing and Rhetoric for English as a Second Language Students (4) GE A1

Writing and stylistic analysis of expository papers. Study and application of techniques of exposition. Critical reading of model essays. Special emphasis on grammar and writing issues appropriate for English as a Second Language students. 4 lectures. **Prerequisite:** ENGL 111, 112, or 113 or consent of instructor. **Next Course in Sequence:** ENGL 145, 148, or 149

ENGL 134 Writing and Rhetoric (4) GE A1

Writing and stylistic analysis of expository papers. Study and application of techniques of exposition. Critical reading of models of effective writing. 4 lectures. **Prerequisite:** Satisfactory score on the English Placement Test. **Next Course in Sequence:** ENGL 145, 148, or 149

ENGL 145 Reasoning, Argumentation, and Writing (4) GE A3

(Also listed as HNRS/SCOM 145) (formerly ENGL 215)

The principles of reasoning in argumentation. Examination of rhetorical principles and responsible rhetorical behavior. Application of these principles to written and oral communications. Effective use of research methods and sources. 4 lectures. **Prerequisite:** Completion of GE Area A1 with a C– or better, or consent of instructor. **Recommended:** Completion of GE Area A2.

ENGL 148 Reasoning, Argumentation and Technical Writing (4) GE A3

(Also listed as HNRS 148) (Replacement for ENGL 218)

The principles of reasoning in technical writing. Discussion and application of rhetorical principles, both oral and written, in technical environments. Study of methods, resources and common formats used in corporate or research writing. 4 lectures. **Prerequisite:** Completion of GE Area A1 with a C– or better, or consent of instructor. **Recommended:** Completion of GE Area A2.

ENGL 149 Technical Writing for Engineers (4) GE A3

(Also listed as HNRS 149) (Engineering replacement for ENGL 218)

The principles of technical writing. Discussion and application of rhetorical principles in technical environments. Study of methods, resources and common formats used in corporate or research writing. 4 lectures. **Prerequisite:** Completion of GE Area A1 with a C– or better, or consent of instructor. **Recommended:** Completion of GE Area A2. For Engineering students only. Crosslisted as ENGL/HNRS 149. Fulfills GE A3.

ENGL 150 Writing Tutorial (1) (CR/NC)

Guided discussion and practice of writing strategies for students seeking support for writing-related coursework and/or the GWR. Weekly, individualized and group sessions with a peer writing consultant offering feedback based on the audience, purpose, and context of a writing task. Total credit limited to 4 units. 1 activity. **Prerequisite:** Completion of GE Area A1 and consent of instructor.

The Graduation Writing Requirement (GWR)

In 1976, the Trustees of the California State University System responded to industry and university demands to address the decline in graduating students' writing skills. They mandated that all students seeking a Bachelor's or Master's degree must "be required to demonstrate their proficiency with regard to writing skills as a requirement for graduation." The Trustees also decreed that assessment of student writing skills take place at the upper-division level. The California State University System thus established the Graduation Writing Assessment Requirement to ensure that students are able to write proficiently before they enter the professional workforce.

At Cal Poly, all students who are seeking a degree, including Master's degrees and teaching credentials, must fulfill the Graduation Writing Requirement (GWR) before a diploma can be awarded. Undergraduate students must complete 90 units before they can attempt to complete the requirement.

Cal Poly has two options for fulfilling the GWR:

1. Pass the Writing Proficiency Exam (WPE), which costs $35 and is given at 9 a.m. on a Saturday early in the fall, winter, and spring quarters. The WPE is a two-hour exam in which students are asked to write a 500–800 word essay that demonstrates their ability to present an argument in an organized manner with fully developed supporting points that are expressed logically and clearly. Students must earn a score of at least eight out of twelve points on the exam in order to fulfill their GWR milestone.

2. Pass a GWR-approved upper-division course with a grade of C or better **AND** receive certification of proficiency in writing based on a 500-word in-class essay. Students in GWR-approved courses will be offered multiple attempts to fulfill the requirements. Students must inform the instructor teaching the course that they are taking it to fulfill the GWR.

   Students can enroll in one of the following NON-GE WRITING courses: English 301, 302, 310, 317, 318, 326; or enroll in one of the following GE C4 LITERATURE courses: 330, 331, 332, 333, 334, 335, 339, 340, 341, 342, 343, 345, 346, 347, 349, 350, 351, 352, 354, 370, 371, 372, 380, or 381.

Appendices

Submitting Your Work to *Fresh Voices*

Dear Writer:

Fresh Voices needs your essays and images!
- Are you proud of essays you wrote in ENGL 133/134?
- Are you interested in photography, painting, or drawing?
- Do you want thousands of next year's students to see your work?
- Do you want to tell future employers that you are PUBLISHED?

If so, submit your work to *Fresh Voices*!
If your essay is selected **you will receive a free copy of the collection and a certificate of achievement.**

What to Submit
- ANY essays you completed in ENGL 133, 134, 102, or 113.
- Original artwork (photography, paintings, drawing, etc.) that could be appropriate for the collection.
- Essays ranging from 2–7 pages in length.
- All citations. We will not consider work that that does not properly cite sources.
- Your draft material (optional). (Consider submitting your drafts—complete with instructor and/or peer comments—along with your final hard copy.

You've Arrived
by Dawn Janke

How to Submit
1. Fill out a release form (posted here: http://english.calpoly.edu/content/fresh-voices-invites-you-submit-your-work).
2. Email a copy of the essay to engl-freshvoices@calpoly.edu. (Please write **"FV"** in the subject line.)
3. Turn in hard copies of your work and the permission form to **47-35F.**

Essays must be received by the last day of finals week in spring quarter to be considered for publication. Please contact me if you have questions. The *Fresh Voices* selection committee looks forward to reading your work!

Dr. Brenda Helmbrecht
Department of English
Director of Writing